Small Law Firm KPIs: How to Measure Your Way to Greater Profits

Mary Juetten

For Customer Assistance Call 1-800-328-4880

Mat #41976147

© 2016 Thomson Reuters
Cover image © Gears and KPI Key Performance Indicator Mechanism used under license from Shutterstock.com

This publication was created to provide you with accurate and authoritative information concerning the subject matter covered; however, this publication was not necessarily prepared by persons licensed to practice law in a particular jurisdiction. The publisher is not engaged in rendering legal or other professional advice and this publication is not a substitute for the advice of an attorney. If you require legal or other expert advice, you should seek the services of a competent attorney or other professional.

For authorization to photocopy, please contact the **Copyright Clearance Center** at 222 Rosewood Drive, Danvers, MA 01923, USA (978) 750-8400; fax (978) 646-8600 or **West's Copyright Services** at 610 Opperman Drive, Eagan, MN 55123, fax (651) 687-7551. Please outline the specific material involved, the number of copies you wish to distribute and the purpose or format of the use.

About the Author

I am a recovering professional accountant and business executive from Canada who went to law school in my forties to become a white collar crime prosecutor. Apparently a strong knowledge of John Grisham's writing and most of Law & Order does not a criminal lawyer make! Instead I added my consulting experience at Price Waterhouse to existing business and new intellectual property knowledge to create a software product that was initially thought to be for entrepreneurs and startups. Over the past three years, we have broadened the platform to include risk assessment, lead generation for numerous providers including accountants, consultants, and attorneys. I started a blog for Traklight about four years ago and now write for Forbes, American Bar Association's Law Technology Today and Law Student Division Before the Bar, and have contributed to Attorney at Work. My second career as a writer has become a combination of my thirty years of accounting, business, consulting, finance, law, technology and time teaching in Canada.

Prior to law school, I worked as a Director of Finance for one of Canada's largest law firms and later in the engineering and construction industry. So the notion of time recording and billing by the hour is not new to me. Plus, my early days in Montreal as an auditor and later as a consultant had me recording my time for years. I worked in the then Big Eight, now the Big Four accounting firms, where I honed my skills around recording and billing hours and the associated metrics. In fact, the audit industry did flat fees way back in the 1980s. Our engagements were all budgeted based on hours needed to complete with an appropriate margin for partner profit. For most of my career, I have worked in the professional services industry and all thirty plus years in large and small business.

In the early 1990s, I worked with key performance metrics within the education system in British Columbia. Applying key performance indicators (KPIs) to the education industry was novel at that time and when I worked at the Canadian law firm, we only had traditional utilization types of measures. When I was with a large Canadian law firm, the concept of budgeting for litigation was a foreign concept to the industry and as I dove into this further, I realized that some of the concepts around the legal industry business development and client satisfaction were still missing from legal KPIs.

One of my university business professors coined the term – start with the end in mind. My personal goal with this book is to provide practical information for solos and small law firms to better measure what they are doing well and what needs to be improved. The plan is to start with existing data and systems to create a simple set of KPIs.

These KPIs will provide the information for attorneys to make data driven decisions to take the necessary actions to improve their practice in terms of business efficiencies and profits but ultimately to create satisfied clients who refer more business. Start small and understand what the metrics are telling you; make changes; and continue to refine as you improve your practice.

Acknowledgments

I want to thank my Traklight team and my Evolve Law co-founder Jules Miller who keep things going while I wrote this book this spring. Also a shout out to the Thomson Reuters folks who answered questions and provided support, including the small law customer survey. I have too many attorney friends to mention individually but over the past couple of years, thank you to all of you who answered my questions about measurement and technology.

Not everyone gets as excited as I do about key performance indicators but a special thanks to my kids, Ashley and Jake, who put up with me talking incessantly about the concepts. And the biggest thank you to my husband who put up with me talking about KPIs on planes, trains, and in automobiles, and who valiantly read the first draft as a non-attorney, non-accountant but a brilliant engineer and project director, who also believes in recording hours!

I can be reached through the Traklight.com website, EvovleLawnow.com, or engage with me on twitter @maryjuetten. #onwards

Introduction

While in law school, I took business law and was very surprised by the number of my fellow classmates who did not understand how to read a balance sheet or the difference between fixed and variable costs. The class taught the law of business but not the business of legal. If you are reading this book and still in law school, take a business class as an elective. That class can be on entrepreneurship or small business management. If you are lucky, there is a legal practice class in law school, and let's hope they are teaching metrics!

Solo attorneys and small law firm lawyers are in business. Law firm partners are small business owners and, in many cases, entrepreneurs. Also, there is no difference between starting a law practice versus hanging out a consulting or an engineering practice shingle. It is not the topic of this book, but these key performance indicator (KPI) principles apply equally to mid-sized and large law firms because they are just bigger businesses delivering legal services.

This is good news for lawyers, particularly solos and smalls. The so-called administrative side of the practice is actually the business side and no different from other startups and small businesses. I am not suggesting that every lawyer run the business aspect of your firm. Quite the opposite. If you are not a trained business person and have no interest, then at a minimum ensure that you hire a good administrative person plus a bookkeeper and tax accountant to ensure you are staying up to date on billing and any tax filings.

However, that bookkeeper or accountant will not be able to run the firm for you. Again, you should be outsourcing the tasks that you are not trained for, but you need a basic understanding of practice metrics that matter.

Also, as in life, you need to understand simple mortgage mechanics, as well as budgeting and accounting basics, to be financially literate. Again, I emphasize that you do not have to earn an accounting designation, but you need to understand how the profits are made and what story the metrics present.

Even better news is that the time and money is not all that matters when you are implementing KPIs. In past years, there has been a shift from focusing on the supply or providing of hours by attorneys to the demand by or needs of the clients. Clients will no longer flood to you merely because you set up shop. Having 100 available hours is useless if clients do not know about you or understand why they need to come to your practice. Client KPIs are the most critical to your firm.

A survey of small law firm KPIs and benchmarking practices was distributed by Thomson Reuters in June 2016 to approximately 690 firms. There were 62 responses, and the questions are listed in APPENDIX F. The responses included 10 solos with about half of the firms under 10 attorneys, about one quarter between 11 and 20 lawyers, and the remaining quarter over 21 attorneys.

Thirty-six, or 58%, of the firms do not use KPIs beyond the traditional number of hours billed. Of those 26 that use some metrics other than hours, only six firms used more than four different metrics, including client satisfaction, cost of client development or acquisition, pipeline dollar value per attorney, aged or overdue accounts receivable, collected billings by attorney, matter profitability, and budget versus actual or opened matters. Of those KPIs, collected billings by attorney is used by 19 respondents; aged or overdue accounts receivable by 15 firms; and matter profitability by 14 firms. Client satisfaction is only measured by three firms, or less than 5% of the total firms surveyed.

The firms were asked for the best indicator of profitability with the following options: take-home amount at month end; actual account balance; matter profitability; and overall firm cost versus pipeline or expected revenue. Fifty-eight responded, and 31, or 53%, use either take-home dollars or the bank balance to measure profitability. Digging a bit deeper, 18 of those 31 firms also do not have KPIs. This includes firms from a solo to over 20 attorneys all with support staff or nonattorneys. This means the majority of firms are looking in the rear view mirror as far as results are concerned. It is both reactive and dangerous to wait until the month or year has passed to evaluate your performance because there is no time for corrective action.

Eighteen of the 58, or 31%, of firms are looking to cost versus budgeted or expected revenue, which is a good start to profitability measurement. Surprisingly, when the same firms were asked if all the timekeepers had financial goals or targets, only 36, or 58%, said yes. Six firms that said that they do not have timekeeper targets but have KPIs. Hours, collections, and billings are used by over half of those 36 firms, yet new clients are only measured by about a quarter of the firms.

When asked if firm profitability has grown over the past two years, 48, or 77%, of the firms said yes, with 16 of those firms citing growth over 20%. However, of the 14 firms without any profit growth, eight did not use KPIs. Specifically, four of the five firms that had two or three attorneys did not use KPIs and had not experienced any increase in profits.

The results for the use of a billing or accounting software product were also surprising, with 50 firms, or 81%, responding in the affirmative. This adoption of practice management software is an important step towards simplifying administrative practices and gathering data for KPIs.

Technology is often shunned by attorneys, and when asked why, it boils down to fear of change, being overwhelmed by the choices, ethical issues, or cost. Although I own a software company that can help lawyers, I do not advocate just adding technology to your practice. It is similar to the past practice of solving business problems by hiring more people. These days, when money is not being made, the answer is too often technology. But until you understand the underlying drivers of profitability and measure the right things, you could be throwing away money by implementing technology too soon. And it goes without saying that once you have systems in place, the return on your investment in that technology must be measured.

KPI knowledge is the power to make informed business decisions for your practice. Ultimately, you are providing valuable services to your clients; therefore, it's critical to measure and monitor your client satisfaction in addition to the cash received.

Everyone's exit strategy is different, but when we turn over or sell the book of business or practice, it would be great to have metrics that show the value of your firm. In other words, a framework for KPIs can not only help you run the practice, but having a solid measurement system will also increase your selling price.

Book Takeaways:

- Learn business basics to run your firm, including how to interpret and evaluate the results.
- Measure inputs, outputs, and activities that matter as a business owner.
- Hire or outsource critical business tasks that are not within your core competencies.
- Use technology with an understanding of business and metrics.
- Start with the end in mind—plan for your exit or retirement.

THOMSON REUTERS PROVIEW™

This title is one of many now available on your tablet as an eBook.

Take your research mobile. Powered by the Thomson Reuters ProView™ app, our eBooks deliver the same trusted content as your print resources, but in a compact, on-the-go format.

ProView eBooks are designed for the way you work. You can add your own notes and highlights to the text, and all of your annotations will transfer electronically to every new edition of your eBook.

You can also instantly verify primary authority with built-in links to WestlawNext® and KeyCite®, so you can be confident that you're accessing the most current and accurate information.

To find out more about ProView eBooks and available discounts, call 1-800-344-5009.

Summary of Contents

Chapter 1.	Why Key Performance Indicators?	
Chapter 2.	Accounting and Budgeting Basics	
Chapter 3.	KPI Framework Overview	
Chapter 4.	Deep Dive KPI 1: Client Development	
Chapter 5.	Deep Dive KPI 2: Cost of Client Acquisition (CAC)	
Chapter 6.	Deep Dive KPI 3: Productivity (PROD)	
Chapter 7.	Deep Dive KPI 4: Profitability (PROF)	
Chapter 8.	Deep Dive KPI 5: Performance (PERF)	
Chapter 9.	Deep Dive KPI 6: Client Experience (CE)	
Chapter 10.	Deep Dive KPI 7: Firm Culture (FC)	
Chapter 11.	Setting Targets	
Chapter 12.	Implementation and Continuous Improvement	
Chapter 13.	Going International	

Appendixes

Appendix A.	Glossary | Translator of Acronyms & Terms
Appendix B.	Comprehensive KPI Listing—KPI 1: Client Development
Appendix C.	Comprehensive KPI Listing—KPI 2: Client Acquisition Costs
Appendix D.	Comprehensive KPI Listing—KPI 3: Productivity
Appendix E.	Comprehensive KPI Listing—KPI 4: Profitability
Appendix F.	Comprehensive KPI Listing—KPI 5: Performance
Appendix G.	Comprehensive KPI Listing—KPI 6: Client Experience
Appendix H.	Comprehensive KPI Listing—KPI 7: Firm Culture
Appendix I.	Implementation Workshop Outline
Appendix J.	Technology Resources

Appendix K. Intersection with Firm Central & KPI Implementation Plan

Appendix L. Small Law Firm KPI/Benchmarking Practices Survey Questions (June 2016)

Appendix M. Resources

Chapter 1

Why Key Performance Indicators?

§ 1:1 Key performance indicators (KPIs) measure outputs that include value for clients
§ 1:2 The lack of understanding about metrics
§ 1:3 Metrics help firms make informed business decisions

§ 1:1 Key performance indicators (KPIs) measure outputs that include value for clients

Key performance indicators (KPIs) or performance metrics for the legal field are starting to receive attention. However, measuring utilization and profit per partner are not the focus of this new KPI framework. Instead, the focus is shifting from measuring inputs like available hours to measuring outputs that include value for clients.

With solos and small firms, the partners must generate new clients, practice law, *and* handle administrative work, including setting targets and evaluating performance. In other words, in small law, the owners are CEOs, CFOs, CTOs, CIOs, and practicing attorneys. The partners are business owners, and the focus should also be on the client's needs and experience, not only the bottom line.

Without clients, you wouldn't have a practice. And yet, plenty of law firms—and businesses in general—fail even when they have an abundance of clients. Why? They fail to measure, track, and act on KPIs.

§ 1:2 The lack of understanding about metrics

In 2015, I was selling the software platform of my company, Traklight, to attorneys and trying to explain opportunity cost and how the technology would save them time evaluating prospective clients and onboarding new clients. I realized that attorneys were not tracking metrics other than utilization rates and that there was a lack of understanding about business concepts like opportunity cost. Sometimes the conversation went like this:

Me: How many hours do you give away a week to prospective clients?
Lawyer: I am not sure. I never record that time.

Me: Well, let's estimate—more than two?
Lawyer: Sure—at least two with all the phone calls and drop-in meetings. Let's say two.
Me: With a billing rate of $350 per hour, that's $700 dollars of potential revenue?
Lawyer: No, I do not actually make the $350; that's my billing rate, so it's not costing me $700.
Me: But if you could bill the hours instead of giving the hours away, you could instead generate $700 of revenue.
Or sometimes it went like this:
Lawyer: I cannot handle any more clients right now and don't really need any leads.
Me: How many clients do you have in the pipeline? How many months' worth of work?
Lawyer: Enough.
Or finally like this:
Me: How much does it cost to secure a new client?
Lawyer: Not sure, why?

I was puzzled that attorneys were not correctly valuing their time and understanding business concepts such as cost of acquiring new clients, opportunity cost, or the importance of time-recording and budgets, even with flat-fee work.

Also, too often performance measurement is seen as a waste of time because it looks to the past. Nothing could be further from the truth. KPIs can and should also be used to evaluate what to do about the future, i.e. what corrective actions should be taken. You may have a good feeling about a month's results based on bustling activity in your office, but the firm's bottom line is not always directly correlated.

§ 1:3 Metrics help firms make informed business decisions

"Data-driven decision making" may be trendy, but it is simply about making informed business decisions. Large law firms have been gathering business intelligence and metrics for years. However, recently some big law firms are looking to move beyond the billable-hour metric. These firms are using billed and collected realization per attorney plus client satisfaction metrics and in some cases building dashboards to provide on-demand metrics. The only financial difference between those big organizations and small law is the number of zeros on the reports. In fact, the process and practice management requirements are basically the same across all professional services.

Lawyers should be able to answer these questions with metrics:

- Do your clients find your services valuable?
- What is the monetary value of each client?
- Do your clients refer additional business?
- How many referrals, and how valuable are they?

The first step is to recognize that clients are the inputs for your business, not the hours available to service those clients. Clients, whether businesses or individuals, are demanding value and accountability. Ultimately, though, every business boils down to whether the cash collected exceeds the money spent.

Chapter 2

Accounting and Budgeting Basics

§ 2:1   Accounting 101
§ 2:2   —Income statement
§ 2:3   —Balance sheet
§ 2:4   —Takeaways
§ 2:5   Budgeting 101
§ 2:6   —Revenue
§ 2:7   —Expenses
§ 2:8   —Fees
§ 2:9   Systems and data

§ 2:1   Accounting 101

You may have attended law school because you wanted to avoid the math involved in engineering and accounting or the blood and gore of medical school but the accounting necessary for KPIs is quite simple. Having a good understanding of the income statement and balance sheet will help with KPIs and running your practice but you do not have to learn the details of trust accounting to master your firm's financial performance. This chapter is an overview of these concepts to help you interpret and evaluate metrics. APPENDIX A contains a glossary of terms to familiarize you with business and law firm standard terminology. Chapter 13 includes information on some differences in those terms if you practice outside of the United States.

§ 2:2   Accounting 101—Income statement

Revenue minus expenses equals net income. As long as that calculation is positive, you are in still in business. Revenue is the earned or, in some cases, the collected fees.

"Cash is King" has been my motto since my early accounting days. It sounds simple, yet when I ask attorneys how many days it takes to collect or how much accounts receivable (A/R) that they have outstanding over 60 days, many do not know.

Commitments to long-term, monthly expenses are called fixed costs, and too many fixed costs can impact your ability to generate cash and keep the doors open. Remembering that you are a small business, being nimble and not entering into too many long term agreements can be helpful if you have a client who is having trouble paying or need to take some time off from your practice. Long term leases of space and equipment are examples of fixed costs.

Costs that you can control and stop at any time are variable costs. Examples would be office supplies; marketing expenses for discretionary events; and month to month rental fees.

Direct and indirect costs are often mixed up with fixed and variable. A cost can be either fixed or variable plus be either direct or indirect. A direct cost of making a product would be the fabric in a dress along with the labor to create the dress. An indirect cost would be the website for selling the dress or the marketing costs for the dress brand. The fabric can be a variable cost because no dress, no fabric purchased. The labor could be fixed if the employee is paid regardless of how many dresses are made. On the other hand, the labor could be variable if the employee is paid based on piece work. However, regardless the revenue for the dress less the direct costs will give you a gross margin to cover your overhead.

Revenue minus direct expenses equals gross margin. Gross margin less indirect expenses, often called overhead, gives net income. You may make a positive gross margin but if your overhead costs are too high, you will lose money.

In a solo practice, you can draw your salary as fixed or variable but likely you have a minimum that you need to draw. When you are working on a case, that effort becomes a direct cost to that particular matter so the matter's revenue minus direct expenses for that matter gives gross margin by matter. We will dive into that concept a bit later but it's important to understand that each matter can have its own mini income statement that gives matter gross margin. In our example below, revenue of $1,100 on Matter XYZ yields a gross margin of $420 or 38% after the direct matter expenses of $680.

In the example below, the revenue is all the revenue collected but the expenses are only those that are billed directly to the matter. In other words, if there was no matter these costs would disappear. Marketing expenses, on the other hand, are not charged to each matter, because they are not direct costs associated with the matter. Instead, marketing is an overhead cost that continues even if one particular matter disappears.

Matter XYZ—Gross Margin

Revenue (billed and collected)	$1,000
Disbursements (billed and collected)	$100
Total Realized Collections = Revenue	**$1,100**
Direct Matter costs:	
Attorney time (from payroll)	$400
Paralegal time (from payroll)	$200
Mailing, filing fees, and copies	$80
Total Direct costs = Expenses	**$680**
Matter Gross Margin	**$420** 38%

==When you have a small business, you know a few numbers off the top of your head and one should be the breakeven burn rate—how much cash you need to generate to cover your monthly committed expenses.== For example, if your firm had the following monthly costs needed to run the firm, then your monthly breakeven burn rate is $28,875. In other words, each month you will burn through $28,875 from either revenue, cash reserves, or a combination of both. This number is also helpful for budgeting.

Monthly Breakeven Burn Rate (Fixed Costs)

Payroll including employee benefits	$22,500
Facilities Rental	$2,500
Professional licenses	$1,750
Software licenses	$1,250
Bank Service Charges	$125
Insurance	$250
Communications & Utilities	$375
Storage Fees	$125
	$28,875

You can be conservative and include some variable cost, particularly if it would take a month or so to get out of some expenses that are variable by giving notice for canceling services. For example, if you had entered into an advertising agreement for $500 per month but you can cancel within 30-day notice pe-

§ 2:2   LAW FIRM KEY PERFORMANCE INDICATORS

riod, you should include that in your monthly breakeven rate unless it is cancelled and the notice period has passed.

§ 2:3   Accounting 101—Balance sheet

Assets minus liabilities equal the owner or partners' equity or the net book value of the practice. Of course that number is not necessarily the value of the practice because it does not include the goodwill of your client list and so on. But like the income statement, if this number is negative, you are in trouble.

Trust accounting touches the income statement and the balance sheet. Managing and staying abreast of the trust account rules is difficult without knowing how to reconcile all the accounts. Luckily it does not impact KPIs. Leave the trust accounting to your bookkeeper unless you can handle it.

Again, cash is king. Know your cash balance (excluding your trust accounts) along with your unbilled time and accounts receivable and understand that converting time to cash is your mission.

Your assets on the balance sheet represent positive value with cash being the most liquid. A quick measure of liquidity is if you look at the balance sheet and you have enough cash on hand (that is not in the trust accounts) to cover a few months of expenses if the accounts receivable stopped being collected.

ASSETS

Current Assets

Checking	$60,000
Client Trust Account	$45,000
Savings	$125,000
Accounts Receivable	$37,500
Work in Progress (Unbilled Time)	$15,000
Prepaid Insurance	$1,500
	$284,000

The total of the monthly breakeven burn rate is $28,875 from our example above and, per the cash balance, excluding client trust accounts, is $185,000. Therefore, about six months can go by before the firm would run out of cash if the accounts receivable were not collected.

We should care about the clients paying their bills (actually invoiced) for work that we have performed. And we want that collected cash to exceed the cash that goes out. Again, we want to be mindful of living month to month, just having enough to pay the monthly expenses, including the solo or partners' draw.

Below is a sample balance sheet for a law firm. ==The assets must always equal the liabilities plus the equity accounts and retained earnings.== Understanding your balance sheet and income statement at a high level is an important business skill for small firm owners.

Balance Sheet as of December 31, 2015

ASSETS
Current Assets

Checking	$60,000
Client Trust Account	$45,000
Savings	$125,000
Accounts Receivable	$37,500
Work in Progress (Unbilled Time)	$15,000
Prepaid Insurance	$1,500
	$284,000

Long Term Assets

Fixed Assets (Furniture, Equipment, Tenant Improvements)	$100,000
Accumulated Amortization	($60,000)
	$40,000
Security Deposits	$2,000
	$42,000

TOTAL ASSETS $326,000

LIABILITIES & EQUITY

Current Liabilities

Accounts Payable	$12,500
Client Trust Liability	$45,000
Payroll Taxes Payable	$2,500
	$60,000

Long Term Liabilities

Bank Loan Payable	$150,000

Equity

Retained Earnings	Equity Accounts	$41,000
Net Income	$75,000

TOTAL LIABILITIES & EQUITY   **$326,000**

The sample income statement below indicates whether the costs are normally fixed or variable costs with a F and V respectively. Each of these expenses and categories can be organized and summarized for what fits your practice and works for you to monitor actual expenses versus budgeted expenses.

Income Statement
Year ended December 31, 2015

Income	Amount
Legal Fees	$550,000
Other Income (Interest Revenue)	$7,500
Late Payment Fees	$500
	$558,000

ACCOUNTING AND BUDGETING BASICS § 2:3

Income Statement (con't)
Year ended December 31, 2015

Expenses	Amount	Fixed or Variable
Advertising	$25,000	V
Amortization	$10,000	F
Bank Service Charges	$1,750	F
Client Costs	$5,000	V
Communications & Utilities	$5,000	F
Computer & Internet Charges	$3,000	F
Continuing Legal Education	$1,500	V
Facilities Rental	$12,000	F
Insurance	$6,000	F
Interest Expense	$5,000	F
Licenses & Permits	$500	F
Marketing	$18,000	V
Meals & Entertainment	$6,000	V
Payroll, Including Employee Benefits	$331,450	F
Professional Dues	$7,500	F
Professional Fees	$10,000	V
Professional Licenses	$3,000	F
Software Licenses	$9,000	F
Storage Fees	$1,800	F
Supplies & Office Expenses	$8,000	V
Taxes	$6,000	V
Travel	$7,500	V
	$483,000	
Net Income	**$75,000**	

§ 2:4 Accounting 101—Takeaways

Unless you collect the cash for billed work, the utilization and billing statistics mean nothing—literally nothing—because collections are everything from a business point of view.

Minimize the fixed costs to the best of your ability to remain nimble in times when you experience billing or collection problems.

§ 2:5 Budgeting 101

A budget can be done many ways, but a common method is to set a revenue target for the year and then divide it by 12 months and then use last year's expenses plus a bit more. Resist the urge to build a budget in that fashion. We refer to that as a top-down budget, and it is not very useful, as you cannot easily tie in your individual efforts to the desired results and you are not put in the position to question each cost element as you build the annual budget.

Take the opportunity to build your firm budget from the ground up, and if you have a larger firm, ask your bookkeeper for some help, but use this "zero-based" budget approach. Start with the basics in terms of how much do you think you and any other team members can generate in terms of revenue and what are the necessary fixed and variable costs to achieve that revenue. It can be as simple as using an Excel sheet to make a wish list of all the spending and then looking at the revenue needed to sustain that level of spending. In other words, you are starting from zero every year.

When calculating revenue, remember that your billing rate is just a means to an end, and the same applies for the flat-fee model. Estimate how much of that revenue is actually collectable. Targets can be based off of last year's results if you have repeat business or a very strong pipeline of work.

As lawyers, it is your decision as to the level of practice to which you aspire. There is no right or wrong answer to how much you wish to work. Decisions around how many team members to have, whether to outsource routine tasks, and so on not only impact your expenses, but also your ability to leverage additional revenue. However, as a solo or small practice, remember that you are a business owner and there is a direct correlation to your effort and income.

Budgeting should be complete before the end of the year so that you are never without a roadmap for measurement. With a KPI framework in place, you can then set your KPI target as part of your budget process.

§ 2:6 Budgeting 101—Revenue

In KISS terms (Keep It Super Simple), how much revenue do X number of clients generate? Do not immediately default to saying, "I bill 100 hours a month at $250, so that is $25,000 per month, and, therefore, my revenue target is $300K." That is just a tricky way of taking $300K and dividing by 12 months.

Under a flat-fee or subscription-fee model, the hour is not the base unit. It becomes a calculation based on number of clients and the revenue per matter or fee estimated for the year.

When looking at your existing clients and potential clients to see what revenue they may generate, a customer relationship management (CRM) system may be helpful. A CRM is not essential (more on CRM below), but it is handy to keep track of your prospective clients and existing clients. You will need to work backwards and forwards to ensure that you have the right number of attorneys, paralegals, and legal assistants to achieve the revenue target.

For budgeting purposes, when we say revenue, it means cash collected in the door. Thus, if you have a history of writing off 10% of your billed amount, factor that into your budgeting process.

§ 2:7 Budgeting 101—Expenses

Fixed expenses are the easiest place to start because these are committed costs based on contracts. Facilities costs such as rent, small equipment rental, telephone and Internet services, and insurance are fixed and easy to predict. Also include software subscriptions or licenses for practice management and research.

Payroll can be fixed or variable, or a combination of both, depending on your agreements with employees and partners. Outsourcing appointment setting or accounting can be a good way of managing the fixed costs of having full-time employees, as can be using technology, but again be careful to evaluate first (see APPENDIX D).

Variable costs include discretionary costs, as opposed to committed costs. You can decide in a given month how much to spend on advertising, meals and entertainment, or marketing.

Knowing your monthly overhead (also known as committed costs or burn rate) is critical to manage your practice. Your monthly overhead includes fixed and often variable costs that are already committed for that month to create the total spend for any given month. That is the target for revenue collected to just breakeven or stay afloat.

§ 2:8 Budgeting 101—Fees

Whether you believe the billable hour as a means for charging for your services are dead or not, most clients appreciate certainty with their fees. That can mean using billable hours but setting a cap on the fees; creating fixed or flat fees; or even a subscription model that is similar to prepaid legal service plans. It is all about having the client avoid surprises and, ultimately, to ensure that you will be paid.

On the budgeting side, this can be daunting for small or solo firms, particularly those working in litigation or on a large project. Again borrowing from other professional service, developing a set of standards for projects or work product can not only help with setting rates. Having budgets based on hours for associates and paralegals provides guidance. It is critical to ensure that all hours are recorded; otherwise, you can end up with incorrect fees.

In the early 2000s, I ran a small software company that created a customized learning management system for oil and gas process operator education. We struggled with a costing model because not everyone would put in all of their time to the actual project. No one wanted to be over budget, so they would work extra hours and not bill to the job. Their time either was as nonbillable or completely unrecorded. It may come as no surprise that compensation and bonuses were tied to utilization rates, so our technical writers, illustrators, and programmers were set on hitting those targets. We were not getting good information on how much it cost for each project. As a result, we were underpricing our products.

The same holds true for the law and fee setting. Communicate and manage client expectations for fees but also remember to have good data when creating your fee structure.

§ 2:9 Systems and data

Before you jump into measurement, take the time to familiarize yourself with your systems and data including mapping out your flow of data based on your workflow.

Every business needs a system of recording revenue and costs plus a budget for those inflows and outflows. APPENDIX A contains a glossary of some of the terms that we will use in this book. Regardless of whether you are accounting for your firm on an Excel spreadsheet or using a computer program like QuickBooks or Xero, be very careful with data input. The old saying "garbage in; garbage out" applies equally to your accounting system and whatever you use for time recording, managing client matters, and so on.

Start with an inventory of your various systems and who collects your data. Common inputs for KPIs come from your practice or case management system, accounting software, scheduling or calendar, and feedback from firm members and clients. Determine if there are any holes between the data you need and the data you can pull from your systems.

It is common to be missing information on the client side, as traditionally measurement has focused on the lawyer's supply of hours and resulting fees. Consider using a customer relationship management system to log your prospective clients. Even as a solo, there are advantages to managing your prospects and existing clients within a database.

Make a list of your data sources and make sure you are comparing similar periods, units, etc. For example, don't compare calendar month information to billing period information if they are different time frames. That said, be careful not to drill too deep on the first pass through your information. If you work with an outsourced bookkeeper, enlist their assistance with the financial metrics.

A few examples of applicable systems are listed below:

Little Technology
Accounting & Payroll—QuickBooks
Email & Calendar—Google
Document Sharing—Dropbox for Business

Technology Enabled
Business Development & Client Relationship Management—Salesforce
Practice Management, Research, Time & Billing, Document Sharing—Firm Central
Accounting & Payroll—QuickBooks
Email & Calendar—Office 365, Including Outlook
Client Feedback—Survey Monkey

Fear not—it is not about the best or most expensive technology, it is about consistent, correct data input. The best system in the world will fail with incorrect information. Firms should focus on starting small with your existing technology, build up your metrics, and then evaluate technology to solve your problems, starting with the biggest pain point.

Chapter 3

KPI Framework Overview

§ 3:1 Introduction to the KPI framework
§ 3:2 Client lifecycle
§ 3:3 Seven areas of measurement in the KPI framework
§ 3:4 Getting started
§ 3:5 Next steps

§ 3:1 Introduction to the KPI framework

Your individual and firm profitability is a choice based on your work or lifestyle. Implementing a KPI framework will allow you to evaluate not only which types of clients are most profitable, but also which value your services the most. Be open to change; there is no point in gathering data and tracking KPIs if you are not willing to evaluate your processes and change. Like anything else, pick a few KPIs from each of the seven areas of metrics in this framework and get started.

KPIs are normally measured at two different levels: firm-wide and individual. Lawyers are not so different from other professionals like accountants and engineers, so the KPI measures and framework are borrowed from other industries. In this book, our overall focus will be on a few simple metrics for each of the seven areas. APPENDIX B contains some additional measurements once the initial framework is up and running.

KPIs are a framework that covers all aspects of your practice, but it is important to understand how the metrics interact. Metrics are measuring inputs, process, and outputs. In other words, to apply a KPI framework, you need to map out your workflow. Since we are focused on a client-centric practice and measurement, let's walk through the various steps with a new client.

§ 3:2 Client lifecycle

Practice areas differ in terms of workflow, billing practices, and more, but we can use a Client Lifecycle approach with some standard functions, as depicted in the diagram below:

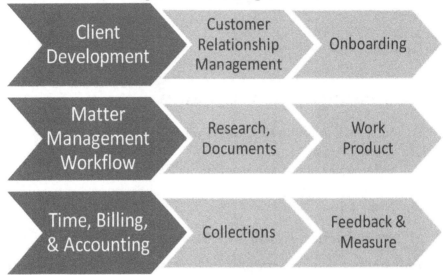

Client Development includes maintaining a pipeline of prospective clients, perhaps with a Client Relationship Management (CRM) system to record activities, including referrals, sources, and specific contact actions, such as interviews. Once a client's conflicts are checked and they are onboarded into the practice management system, the legal work begins.

Depending on the practice area, workflow can include: research, calendaring, docketing, filing, court, document management, document assembly, project management, purchasing, advising, and any other tasks.

The accounting and payroll systems are normally separate systems from the practice management system that may include time and billing. Interactions with clients can be managed very efficiently through a client portal and also electronic document signing software. Collections, measuring results, and obtaining feedback round out the client lifecycle.

§ 3:3 Seven areas of measurement in the KPI framework

The KPI framework is divided into the seven areas as listed below, and the book has a chapter devoted to the metrics associated with each area:
- Client Development;
- Client Acquisition Cost;
- Productivity;
- Profitability;

- Performance;
- Client Experience; and
- Firm Culture.

Client development is acquiring new clients or selling additional services to existing clients. Client Acquisition Cost measures the often overlooked time and money spent on generating new business. Productivity looks at the timekeepers' efficiency and leverage, whereas Profitability measures the return for the owners, including the costs and other ratios. Performance moves from the firm to the individual timekeepers' results. Client Experience is client satisfaction or feedback. Finally, Firm Culture is the measurement of the health of the firm workplace.

Although the firm workflow starts with the development of new business, repeat clients or upselling to existing clients is the best client-development strategy. Also having satisfied clients refer their connections to your firm is economical. Therefore, the workflow does not end with each engagement, but rather is a continuous cycle. Below are the seven areas of measurement in the KPI framework inserted into a circle symbolizing continuity.

§ 3:3   LAW FIRM KEY PERFORMANCE INDICATORS

The full listing of the metrics associated with each of the seven areas above are contained in APPENDIX B. Chapters 4 to 10 include a deep dive into seven firm examples, one for each KPI area in the framework.

§ 3:4 Getting started

Start small and collect data from the past year to establish a baseline set of data. For some firms, you could run the framework on one lawyer's practice or practice group to start. Specifically go back one year at a high level for all areas of measurement and see if there are any outliers or strange results. For example, if your collections metrics show a large dip in a certain month, then dig deeper. Otherwise, the prior year data will be a valuable baseline as you set budgets and targets, and measure your results.

It is impossible to measure what is not recorded or tracked. KPIs should not be a separate project outside of the practice management workflow or system. Ideally, your case or practice management system should have a KPI dashboard. Most likely you will have to create an Excel workbook that draws from your various systems. It is best to have your regular reporting integrate with any Excel files, so that you are not doubling your data input. Building in a KPI framework is a change management process, and it will only succeed with proper support and an actual process to capture and review the data against targets.

§ 3:5 Next steps

We will now dive into the details of the seven areas of the KPI framework. Each of the following chapters uses a different size firm practicing a specific type of law as an example to illustrate that the KPIs can be applied to any type of practice. In fact, this framework can be used outside of the United States with some adjustments to terminology (see APPENDIX A).

We use the terms "attorney" and "paralegal" to include the following:

> Attorneys—attorneys, associates, and Limited License Legal Technicians—anyone capable of practicing directly with clients.
> Paralegals—employees working on clients under the supervision of attorneys or associates.

We are trying to isolate the use of paralegals versus attorneys, but this can be adjusted for your situation. Finally, each of the seven deep-dive chapters can standalone, and, therefore, some basic information around frequency, data sources, and technology is repeated in each for completeness.

Chapter 4
Deep Dive KPI 1: Client Development

§ 4:1 Introduction
§ 4:2 KPI 1—Client development (CD) summary
§ 4:3 Data and sources
§ 4:4 Background
§ 4:5 Firm example: FAMILY CD
§ 4:6 —First quarter results
§ 4:7 —Full year results
§ 4:8 —Prior year data points
§ 4:9 Technology to assist with client development KPIs
§ 4:10 Common mistakes or pitfalls

§ 4:1 Introduction

Although I did once have an attorney tell me that he had enough clients for years of future work, I believe that developing new business is difficult for most lawyers. Measurements around Client Development (CD) can identify and alleviate frustrations around new business development with a systematic approach that isolates problem areas. I encourage you to simultaneously work on KPI 2: Client Acquisition Cost (CAC), as these two measures can help with the bottom line and ensuring you pursue the right clients.

§ 4:2 KPI 1—Client development (CD) summary

The first KPI area on Client Development (CD) contains four metrics as outlined in the table below, and APPENDIX B, Comprehensive KPI Listing—KPI 1: Client Development, presents the information in table format with formulas.

1-CD Metrics	Calculation	Frequency**
1-CD (a): New Client Conversion Rate (%)	Number of new clients divided by number of potential clients to yield a percentage.	Monthly
1-CD (b): Client Referral Rate (%)	Number of new clients referred by existing clients divided by total new clients to yield a percentage.	Annually or could be quarterly, depending on the client volume
1-CD (c): Prospect Client Pipeline (#)	Total number of prospective clients listed on the pipeline divided by total attorneys (and paralegals if they work directly for clients).	Monthly
1-CD (d): Adjusted Prospect Pipeline ($)	Total dollar value of the prospective clients' matters on the pipeline adjusted for likelihood of success divided by total attorneys (and paralegals in some cases*) to yield a dollar value.	Monthly

   * If the paralegals are supporting the attorneys and not generating their own work, you could include the number of paralegals into the calculation. However, if you are consistent in comparing this measure of the dollars in the pipeline to the Profitability targets for Attorneys, then you just need to always compare like calculations. There is more on this below in the firm example.

   ** We recommend that KPIs are tracked regularly, either monthly, quarterly, or annually, once fully implemented. In the early stages of adoption, try to collect as much data as possible monthly and do an assessment at the end of the first quarter, including a comparison to the prior year. Some metrics will lend themselves to monthly measurement, while others will be naturally quarterly or annually. However, each firm's situation will be different, and there is simply no right or wrong approach to measurement; therefore, the frequencies listed in table are only recommendations or examples.

§ 4:3 Data and sources

Interactions with potential clients need to be captured from the beginning. By the time you are completing a client intake form, it is too late. At the point of client onboarding, you will no longer be able to gather information on the unsuccessful pursuits, or those who did not become clients. Data needs to be captured at the point of first contact or connection for all client leads plus information on referral sources; assessment or triage numbers for all types of interviews; and pipeline information, including client names, value, and likelihood of success.

First connections | Client leads—Website contact enquiries, phone calls, e-mails, and visits need to be captured in a log to generate the number of potential clients. That log can be manual, on an Excel spreadsheet, or created from a CRM or practice management system. More on technology options below in our firm example.

Referral sources—You need to ask every potential client how they heard about your practice right away—that should be part of any website contact form, and the person fielding the calls for your firm should have this as part of the script or process. If you are using a virtual assistant, you can have your specific questions built into that script. These can be logged manually and entered weekly or monthly into spreadsheet. Any customer relationship management (CRM) system should have the ability to capture and create reports on this information.

Referrals should be categorized as follows (plus anything that is specific to your practice setup):

- Existing or past clients;
- Advertisements;
- Attorneys within the firm;
- External attorneys;
- Events;
- Writing or speaking;
- Press coverage;
- Paid referral networks; and
- Other (with a description).

Assessment or Triage Numbers—In-person interviews, phone calls, forms, or technology on your website, whatever your process for evaluating potential clients, there needs to be a log of the number of these events and how much time is spent by whom (this is part of the nonbillable business or client development time that needs to be captured). A calendaring or practice management system may have the capability to generate a report of the number of events, and the time keeping system can supply the hours spent with potential clients.

New clients—Clients who have never been your clients or clients of your firm should be tracked as the client is onboarded into the practice management system or added to the accounting system if there is not a practice management system in place. Count only one client even if they end up with multiple matters. In other words, you are looking to count the number of brand new clients because you will compare that to the number of potential clients that you spend time assessing.

Pipeline—Similar to the first connections or leads, a pipeline is a listing of all the potential clients or leads that attorneys are working on. Most CRMs have this, but it can also be generated from an Excel listing of all the first connections. In sales, it is common to classify different types of potential clients in a systematic way, starting from suspect:

- **Suspect**—Someone has just contacted your firm and you are not certain if they are a fit for your practice;
- **Prospect**—Initial information, however gathered, indicates that this suspect is a candidate for your services;
- **Lead**—Often referred to as qualified, the prospect is now a very real possibility for your firm. These are your Potential Clients for KPIs;
- **Closed**—From a lead status, the next phase is that either the business is won or lost, so you mark the prospect as closed on your pipeline. The win becomes a *New Client* for KPI purposes;
- **Paused**—There is the possibility that the client needs more time to decide or postpones the work, so there is a paused category also.

These labels are just one version of what is called the sales funnel. Do not get hung up in the terminology or number of categories. For example, if you wish to simplify down to two choices: either lead or not, it will still work. However, ensure that the number of leads and the resulting wins and losses are tracked with the referral sources, as this will help you analyze your business development process once you have the KPI results.

Pipeline Value & Likelihood of Success—First, place a potential estimated value for the potential known work beside each lead. The likelihood of success can be calculated by estimating the "go" and the "get" as described below and multiplying the two factors together.

- **Go**—the likelihood that the client will go ahead with their request for legal representation or services.
- **Get**—the firm will be awarded the legal work.

Usually 25%, 50%, 75%, and 100% are used for each of "go" and "get" to simplify the process and the results. Depending on your practice, it may be difficult to place a value on all the leads, but it is only an estimate and you can refine over time.

Attorneys—the number of attorneys or paralegals, depending on your structure, that will be fulfilling the work in the pipeline. The pipeline should be shared firm-wide but can be isolated down to a single attorney, practice area, or a department within a firm.

§ 4:4 Background

The KPI framework starts with client measures because without new clients there is no business for your firms. Many clients now search for a do-it-yourself (DIY) legal service, particularly millennials. Even though there are staggering figures about how many Americans are in need of legal services, actually winning clients is still difficult. However, your current clients are the best source of new revenue because it is much easier and less expensive to upsell to your existing clients or have them provide referral business. Most lawyers provide additional or follow-on services. For example, a business lawyer might help with a contract and then spot some more issues needing attention, or a client's will or child support agreement needs a review every few years. Criminal defense lawyers often are retained on word-of-mouth referrals, and, of course, there are paid referral networks.

Creating new business is forward-looking but relies on collecting historical data as described under Data and Sources. Before we expand upon the theoretical information on the four Client Development KPIs, let's discuss the concept of a sales pipeline. Using a system to manage the often massive amount of information on your clients is not a new concept for the law. However, centralizing and sharing that information between lawyers is a different approach. The idea of sharing the pipeline and information to create additional opportunities within small firms should be exciting. Your clients do not wish to have to talk to more than one person to explain their story. My personal experience with small firms is that without a good practice management and CRM system, I have had to reexplain my needs and backstory repeatedly within the same partnership! That was frustrating for not only me as a client, but also for the two lawyers involved.

§ 4:5 Firm example: FAMILY CD

FAMILY CD is a family law practice run by attorney Chris Dunn, who has one paralegal, Cassidy Davis. Chris has been practicing for about 10 years and is considering changing over to flat fees, but at this time, he still bills his clients based on hours. Most of Chris' practice is focused on middle-class divorces and the related child support work, but recently he has represented a couple of prominent local business people in some high-profile cases. Chris has been fielding calls, and Cassidy has been swamped with contact forms, but the billings from the practice have not been growing in the last three months of the prior year. In fact, some weeks it seems like Cassidy does not have enough client work.

FAMILY CD has a website with a contact form, and Chris' mobile phone number is on the home page of the website. He lists Cassidy's firm email address on the website for those who do not wish to fill in the contact form or call him. Although he lists the firm's office address on the home page, it is very rare for a client to just pop in. The website contact form asks for basic personal information and reason for contacting FAMILY CD, and that information goes to Cassidy.

The computer systems in place are very simple. Chris uses paid Google Applications for email, as well as document storage and sharing; a simple standalone case management platform, including a time and billing system, both cloud based; and Microsoft Office 365, including Excel for lists. Accounting, payroll, and billings are done by a local bookkeeper remotely. Chris does not have a customer relationship management (CRM) platform.

Chris has decided to implement KPIs to help him better understand his client development process. Some of the information needed for the four CD KPIs is readily available. Chris creates an Excel workbook to manage the data input for KPIs and enlists Cassidy's help to fill in the information. However, before Chris can pull data from his system, he makes a few decisions on the approach, as follows:

i. **Define a Potential Client**—a simple inquiry is likely not enough, even if it comes from a website form completion. Chris decides that anyone that he or Cassidy spent any amount of time with, other than a cursory look, should be counted as a Potential Client. However, even if they decide that they are not a fit for FAMILY CD, Chris will attempt to refer them elsewhere.

ii. **Simplify Pipeline**—Chris wants a simple pipeline to manage, and, as he is only one attorney, he will classify Potential Clients as Leads, which then will become either Won or Lost. The pipeline was never formalized because Chris just used his calendar to track his tasks, and that included meetings with potential clients.

iii. **Pricing & Go|Get Assumptions**—Chris reviews his billings from the last six months and decides to divide his clients into four types of client matters and use a ballpark revenue figure for each type based on size of matter:

Deep Dive KPI 1: Client Development § 4:6

    a. Small—$1,500,
    b. Medium—$5,000,
    c. Large—$10,000,
    d. Intense—$25,000.

Chris tries to pull together the data from the prior year and realizes that he has the following gaps in his client development process in addition to not having a formal prospective client pipeline listing.

Potential Client Sources

Chris does not track where the clients come from—Are they referred by previous or existing clients? Was the referral as a result of paid advertising, press coverage, or speaking at the local Chamber of Commerce?

Action: Chris adds a drop-down box to the website with the query, "How did you find out about FAMILY CD?" Cassidy will always look to see if that part of the contact form was completed, and Chris will always ask that question on any initial phone calls from the website.

Potential Client Interview Information

Cassidy has a few questions to ask when she follows up by phone to the website inquiries, but she does not ask about the details of the case. She puts that information into Chris' personal calendar for him to have either a 30-minute call or an hour in-person meeting with the potential client. There is no entry to the FAMILY CD calendar for these meetings to be tracked.

Action: Create a firm calendar that has all the client interviews listed in one color so that Cassidy can count and manage them on one calendar.

Targets

Chris does not set anything other than an overall revenue target for the firm. He will just put in some targets based on his gut feeling to start and then refine after the first quarter.

Action: Set initial targets and review after three months and every subsequent quarter.

Therefore, Chris will be unable to produce KPIs for the prior year; however, he should still gather what data he can for the past 12 months, in this case 2015. Those data points can be useful as comparisons as shown below.

§ 4:6 Firm example: FAMILY CD—First quarter results

Chris completes the first three months of 2016, including a

pipeline calculation for the prospects outstanding at the end of the month.

PIPELINE EXAMPLE—MARCH 2016				
FAMILY CD	$ Value	Go	Get	Adjusted Value
Client 1	$1,500	50%	50%	$375
Client 2	$5,000	75%	100%	$3,750
Client 3	$5,000	75%	50%	$1,875
Client 4	$10,000	100%	100%	$10,000
Client 5	$1,500	100%	25%	$375
Client 6	$25,000	25%	100%	$6,250
TOTAL	$48,000			$22,625

This month was Chris' third time completing a pipeline. Initially, in January, after applying the go|get percentages, Chris' pipeline was $50,000, which turned out to be unrealistic. Also, for the first three months, he would only create or update the pipeline spreadsheet at the end of the month by looking at a list of outstanding prospects on his computer task list. Starting with the potential client inquiries in April, Chris asked Cassidy to maintain a pipeline Excel document to be shared and updated with all the inquiries that pass the initial first review and become a lead on the pipeline. Being a lead on the pipeline means that the prospect is a potential client and that a phone call or in-person meeting will be scheduled.

Once per week on Fridays, Chris and Cassidy will spend about 15 minutes reviewing the pipeline to make sure that all the information is updated and matches the scheduled calls and meetings. The pipeline numbers in the one Excel document can be linked to the overall KPI Excel workbook for the firm within their Google documents.

1-CD (a): New Client Conversion Rate for the first three months of 2016:

FAMILY CD 2016			
	Jan	Feb	Mar
1-CD(a) New Client Conversion Rate (%)	5%	20%	11%
TARGET New Client Conversion Rate (%)	50%	50%	50%
Number of Potential Clients	20	15	18
Input—client calls	15	3	8
Input—in-person meetings	5	12	10
Input—total new clients (matters)	1	3	2

Chris set a target of 50% for his new client conversion rate. For every two people that Chris will speak to, one will be a client. Since Chris did not have a recorded track record of how successful he was in the past, he thought this was the best estimate of what had been happening in the past.

Chris was not being consistent between the number of calls recorded as potential clients and whether he actually thought that the call would yield a paying matter. Sometimes he put down that he spoke with someone when he was only referring them to another attorney.

After looking at the first three months, Chris still kept the same target but made some process changes.

 i. Changed the contact number on the website from his cell phone number to the firm number.
 ii. Added in an area on the contact form to have clients describe their needs and provide more information on their legal issues, i.e. child support or divorce.
 iii. Created a list of qualifying questions and a script of services for Cassidy to either follow-up on the contact forms or ask when clients called in to the firm phone.
 iv. Created a referral list so that Cassidy referred the clients that were not even potential FAMILY CD clients such that Chris neither spent any time with those clients nor recorded them as calls.

1-CD (b): Client Referral Rate for the first quarter in 2016:

FAMILY CD 2016			
	Jan	Feb	Mar
1-CD(b) Client Referral Rate (%)	NA	NA	33%
TARGET—Client Referral Rate (%)	NA	NA	33%
Input—new clients referred by existing or former clients	1	1	0
Total new clients (linked to original)	1	3	2

Again, Chris set an arbitrary target of one in three existing or former clients making a referral. That number was based on an educated guess of how many of his clients would know someone needing his services. Cassidy thought that this target should be lower, given the number of family lawyers in town.

Chris was right on target for the first quarter, but he decided to lower the target for the remainder of 2016 because his focus for the rest of the year would be on more of the larger clients and he had only done two large and one intense case in all his years running FAMILY CD.

1-CD (c): Prospect Client Pipeline for the first three months of 2016:

FAMILY CD 2016			
	Jan	Feb	Mar
1-CD (c) Prospect Client Pipeline (#)	5	4	6
TARGET - Prospect Client Pipeline (#)	10	10	15
Input - number of prospective clients (leads)	5	4	6
Input - number of attorneys	1	1	1

As mentioned above, Chris made some significant changes to his pipeline in terms of only putting real potential clients into the spreadsheet. In April, Chris and Cassidy also decided to spend about one hour at the beginning of each week going over the pipeline and any action items or questions from the prior week. They decided upon the first of the week because there were website inquiries over the weekend and Cassidy was trying to return all the requests by noon on Mondays. Chris added in some wording on their website indicating that someone from the firm would be back in touch within 24 hours during the week and by the end of Monday if it was a weekend inquiry.

1-CD (d): Adjusted Prospect Pipeline for the first three months of 2016:

FAMILY CD 2016			
	Jan	Feb	Mar
1-CD(d) Adjusted Prospect Pipeline ($)	$50,000	$27,750	$22,625
TARGET—Adjusted Prospect Pipeline ($)	$20,000	$20,000	$20,000
Input—Adjusted Value	$50,000	$27,750	$22,625
Input—number of attorneys	1	1	1

Pipeline calculations were challenging for Chris, which is not unusual. These are estimates from the value of the clients' matters to the likelihood of being hired and so on. It is an art and takes practice. Getting the right data into the model consistently is a good start, and refining the results over time will pay off in the long run.

§ 4:7 Firm example: FAMILY CD—Full year results

Exhibit 1 at the end of the chapter contains the full year results for the Client Development KPI. Chris' process changes for client inquiries and initial calls or meetings seemed to have paid off. Initially, in April, the total numbers dipped, but that was because Chris was no longer counting the referrals he was making as potential clients. He also freed himself up to focus on building up the pipeline. He was able to leverage Cassidy's time to triage the calls for him, and based on his high-profile cases, he was receiving many large and intense potential client inquiries.

Cassidy was able to direct those more valuable potential clients to Chris for meetings or calls and was able to provide the information on the small and medium services by following the written scripts created by Chris. Although in April the firm only added two new matters, the value of those matters were $1,500 and $25,000. Chris decided to only do in-person meetings for the large and intense potential clients. He would then have Cassidy field the small leads over the phone within 15 minutes, and he would handle the medium leads with phone calls instead of meetings.

Chris grew the case workload in July and August so much that he needed to bring on an associate. Chad Daniels started in September and focused on legal work, working with Cassidy, in addition to onboarding the small and medium-sized clients.

As far as client referrals, not only has Cassidy been tracking all the referral sources, the firm has sponsored some client appreciation events and ensures that handwritten thank you notes are sent to anyone who refers a client.

The client pipeline is healthier, and there is a focus on having the right mix of leads. A year's worth of experience in terms of go|get estimations has the new client results more in line with the adjusted pipeline. In August, Chris added in typical fee ranges for his different types of cases on the website near the contact us form. Chris is now researching a CRM system to help share the information within firm between the three professionals and streamline the process. The CRM should create the firm pipeline within the system and export that information to the practice management system.

There was a bit of drop in qualified prospects in terms of absolute numbers between August and September, mainly because the leads are now shared by two attorneys with the addition of Chad. From a dollar perspective the pipeline is growing, even when divided by the two attorneys, with the exception of December. For next year, Chris will adjust the targets for December, as it is historically a slow month. Chris will focus on the discovering right number and value of clients within the pipeline to create a steady revenue stream for the firm.

Deep Dive KPI 1: Client Development

§ 4:7

Exhibit 1—Client Development Family CD 2016

CLIENT DEVELOPMENT

FAMILY CD 2016	Jan	Feb	Mar	Apr	May	June	July	Aug	Sept	Oct	Nov	Dec
1-CD(a) New Client Conversion Rate (%)	5%	20%	11%	20%	30%	38%	65%	41%	43%	34%	19%	26%
TARGET New Client Conversion Rate (%)	50%	50%	50%	50%	50%	50%	50%	50%	50%	50%	50%	50%
Number of Potential Clients	20	15	18	10	23	24	17	27	28	38	26	34
Input - client calls	15	3	8	6	17	16	15	25	20	28	14	22
Input - in-person meetings	5	12	10	4	6	8	2	2	8	10	12	12
Input - total new clients	1	3	2	2	7	9	11	11	12	13	5	9

FAMILY CD 2016	Jan	Feb	Mar	Apr	May	June	July	Aug	Sept	Oct	Nov	Dec
1-CD(b) Client Referral Rate (%)			33%			22%			24%			30%
TARGET - Client Referral Rate (%)			33%			25%			25%			25%
Input - new clients referred by existing or former clients	1	1	0	1	1	2	2	1	5	2	1	5
Total new clients (linked to original)	1	3	2	2	7	9	11	11	12	13	5	9

FAMILY CD 2016	Jan	Feb	Mar	Apr	May	June	July	Aug	Sept	Oct	Nov	Dec
1-CD (c) Prospect Client Pipeline (#)	5	4	6	7	10	12	15	18	11	17.5	16	13.5
TARGET - Prospect Client Pipeline (#)	10	10	15	15	25	25	30	30	30	30	30	30
Input - number of prospective clients (leads)	5	4	6	7	10	12	15	18	22	35	32	27
Input - number of attorneys	1	1	1	1	1	1	1	1	2	2	2	2

FAMILY CD 2016	Jan	Feb	Mar	Apr	May	June	July	Aug	Sept	Oct	Nov	Dec
1-CD(d) Adjusted Prospect Pipeline ($)	$50,000	$27,750	$22,625	$16,225	$18,400	$43,750	$24,000	$32,475	$16,850	$21,000	$37,500	$18,375
TARGET - Adjusted Prospect Pipeline ($)	$20,000	$20,000	$20,000	$20,000	$20,000	$20,000	$20,000	$20,000	$27,500	$27,500	$27,500	$27,500
Input - Adjusted Value	$50,000	$27,750	$22,625	$16,225	$18,400	$43,750	$24,000	$32,475	$33,700	$42,000	$75,000	$36,750
Input - number of attorneys	1	1	1	1	1	1	1	1	2	2	2	2

§ 4:8 Firm example: FAMILY CD—Prior year data points

In 2015, Chris did not have any complete data sets for the four metrics and only was able to pull together the total new clients for each month in 2015. That was helpful to explain the dip in November and December of 2016. After months of increased new client matters to a peak of 13 new matters in October 2016, the total new matters in the last two months were five and nine only.

By reviewing the same period in 2015, Chris saw that the same dip occurred in November and December 2015, with only two and three new matters versus five in October. Going forward, Chris now has a complete data set for 2016 to move into 2017.

§ 4:9 Technology to assist with client development KPIs

Properly implemented technology can not only assist with data collection and reduce duplication of tasks but also improve and streamline law firm workflow or process. Some of the technology that can be used to assist with client development KPIs includes:

- Excel—to avoid problems with various versions of the same spreadsheet, use a safe shared drive or server, and create links between different workbooks and sheets to simplify data input.
- Legal Practice Management (LPM)—the number of new clients and matters should be generated from the LPM, and an integrated calendar can help gather the statistics onphone calls and meetings.
- Customer Relationship Management (CRM)—a pipeline can usually be created within a CRM, and the clients' information can be shared on an ongoing basis.
- Appointment Setting—software programs or virtual assistants can help with setting meetings with prospective clients.
- Calendar—many LPMs and calendars can integrate and synchronize to pass data on appointments and tasks.

A nonexhaustive list of technology resources is in APPENDIX D.

§ 4:10 Common mistakes or pitfalls

The above firm example and other experiences give rise to lessons learned that are set out below as common mistakes or pitfalls to avoid:

§ 4:8   DEEP DIVE KPI 1: CLIENT DEVELOPMENT

- Counting every call or inquiry as a potential client or lead for KPI purposes. Unless you truly believe that the person is a fit for your practice AND you are not going to spend any significant time with them, they should be excluded.
- Being too busy practicing and doing administrative work to recognize the benefits of involving your associates, paralegals, and assistants in the client development process by providing some structured questions or scripts.
- Worrying about target setting too soon. Create some data and review your targets quarterly in the first year and, in some cases, monthly.
- Not adapting the KPIs for your firm's situation. For example, if your main source of referrals is a paid source and not existing clients, then adapt 1-CD(b) Client Referral Rate to be Referral Network rate. Change out the formula as follows: Number of New Clients referred by Referral Network divided by the total New Clients.
- Laser focusing on one metric. All these metrics work together in a system. If you focus on maximizing the number of clients that you onboard without regard to the different size or revenue from those clients, you may be wasting effort. For example, if Chris did not differentiate between his pursuit of a $25,000 client versus a $1,500 client, he would risk spending too much time on the absolute number of new clients versus the value of these clients to his practice.

In the next chapter we continue to examine client metrics with the second KPI—Cost of Client Acquisition—using a solo intellectual property (IP) lawyer as an example.

Chapter 5

Deep Dive KPI 2: Cost of Client Acquisition (CAC)

§ 5:1 Introduction
§ 5:2 KPI 2—Cost of client acquisition (CAC) summary
§ 5:3 Data and sources
§ 5:4 Background
§ 5:5 Firm Example: CAC IP
§ 5:6 Firm example: CAC IP—First quarter results
§ 5:7 —Full year results
§ 5:8 —Prior year data points
§ 5:9 Technology to assist with client acquisition cost KPIs
§ 5:10 Common mistakes or pitfalls
§ 5:11 Small firms

§ 5:1 Introduction

The client acquisition cost concept is borrowed from software as a service and other industries where a substantial amount of effort is placed on understanding the path to revenue. As mentioned previously, the referrals from existing and current clients are the best place to start, as often the time to win that new business is less than for someone who is not familiar with your firm.

However, upselling additional but necessary services to existing clients is usually less time-consuming and, therefore, more economical than finding new clients, even referrals. All of this is quite theoretical until you start to put some numbers to your client acquisition costs. Remember this KPI goes hand-in-hand with the first set of KPIs on Client Development (CD).

§ 5:2 KPI 2—Cost of client acquisition (CAC) summary

The second KPI area on Client Acquisition Cost (CAC) contains four metrics as outlined in the table below, and APPENDIX B Comprehensive KPI Listing—KPI 2: Client Acquisition Cost, presents the information in table format with formulas.

2—CAC Metrics	Calculation	Frequency*
2-CAC (a): Client Acquisition Cost (CAC) ($)	Advertising, sales, and marketing spend plus the opportunity cost of the staff and lawyer time divided by the number of new clients.	Monthly
2-CAC (b): Upsell Rate (%)	The number of new matters with existing clients divided by all new matters.	Monthly
2-CAC (c): Client Lifetime or Annual Value (CLV) ($)	Lifetime cumulative revenue for each client. To start you can create an annual number by dividing cumulative annual revenue for the firm by the number of clients served, or you can create CLV for different types of clients, both based on historical data.	Annually
2-CAC (d): CLV to CAC Ratio (ratio)	The 2- CAC(c) CLV is divided by the calculated CAC for each client.	Annually

*We recommend that KPIs are tracked regularly, either monthly, quarterly, or annually, once fully implemented. In the early stages of adoption, try to collect as much data as possible monthly and do an assessment at the end of the first quarter, including a comparison to the prior year. Some metrics will lend themselves to monthly measurement, while others will be naturally quarterly or annually. However, each firm's situation will be different, and there is simply no right or wrong approach to measurement; therefore, the frequencies listed in the table are only recommendations or examples.

§ 5:3 Data and sources

Costs and revenues are two main types of data collected for the CAC KPI. The costs include not only direct costs, like sales, marketing, and event sponsorship, but also indirect costs of the time spent by attorneys and staff pursuing new clients.

Also, similar to KPI 1: Client Development, it is important to note both the number of brand new clients and also the additional work or matters for existing clients. Revenue by client by matter is something that most systems already track, but we will be looking for the lifetime value of clients, which can span more than one year, depending on the type of practice.

Direct CAC costs—Most accounting systems allow you to

customize their different accounts, and most firms will already have accounts for advertising, sales, or marketing efforts. You are looking for costs that are solely for selling and client development. For example, sponsoring an event for prospective clients would be included but attending a bar association meeting would not be considered a cost of client acquisition. The former should be in the sales and marketing account, but the latter would be under professional development.

Confirm with your bookkeeper which accounts should be included in the direct costs of client acquisition.

Indirect CAC costs—The salaries and time spent on developing new and existing client business needs to be included in the CAC calculation, but the data is not necessarily sourced from the payroll system. It depends on whether the person involved in the client development has a billable-hour or client-service role.

If a lawyer, paralegal, legal assistant, or administrative person normally bills to client matters, then the cost of any time spent on client development or acquisition should be included at their billing rate, not their hourly wage.

If the employee does not bill out for their time, then their time can be included at their wages plus benefits.

For example, if a lawyer gives away an hour consultation and normally bills $200 per hour, the cost of that consultation is $200 which could have been earned if they were billing someone else during that time period. The amount included in CAC is not the lawyer's salary for the hour but the revenue or opportunity lost by giving away the potentially billable time. This concept of opportunity cost is important when deciding how much time to spend with a prospective new client vs the potential revenue from that client.

The time and billing system needs to capture the client development time as a nonbillable in order to run a monthly report of all nonbillable time and apply the billing rates to give the dollar value. Another approach is to include all the billable time in hours and apply an average billing rate for the timekeepers involved in the client development. The latter is not as precise but particularly if you are looking at gathering data for a prior year or for the first time, this approach adopts the KISS (Keep it Super Simple) principle and is sufficient to get started.

One code for all nonbillable client development can be used if you are lumping all that time together and not trying to identify the hours spent pursuing a particular client. For example, if at the end of the month, one lawyer spends a total of 21 hours securing seven new clients, the KISS approach will average that out as three hours per new client pursuit.

Both direct and indirect costs are aggregated to create an average CAC by new client for the firm. To calculate the actual CAC for each client, see the section at the end of the firm example, titled "Adaption for Small Firms."

Client revenue– Client revenue will come from the practice management system or the accounting system, depending on how your billing is set up. To calculate individual lifetime client revenue, you need to pull cumulative revenue by client.

For firms where the engagement might be limited to one case or project that starts and finishes within a couple of months, the data should be easy to pull together within the current year. If your firm has long standing clients where you are not closing out the engagement but instead represent businesses or families for years, you will wish to pull data from as far back as practical.

The CAC KPI includes a comparison between the lifetime revenue for a client and the cost of the effort to secure that client revenue. Total client revenue over the lifetime of the engagement for each client is our ultimate goal.

For this metric challenges often arise when trying to gather data for the first time. First, there may be gaps if you have to go back years for the cumulative client revenue and you have nothing to compare that revenue with. In other words, you did not have systems in place to gather the cost to acquire that client back then. Another challenge occurs when measuring the client lifetime revenue for brand new clients in the current year. You may not know how much revenue will come from the new engagement at the time when the work is won.

There are several ways to tackle these issues to ensure you are generating meaningful comparisons:

- The revenue for the older clients can be used as a proxy until you build up more information on the new clients. You can divide your clients into various types or standards. For example, if you are doing wills & estates work, perhaps you have two or three sizes of matters—simple, single-person will; family will; and complex trust work. If you look at the results of the revenue generated for your top 30 cases over the past three years, you should get a sense of the different ranges of lifetime value from clients. Until you have actual numbers for the current year, then use those numbers as proxies, either as one number or by the different types of work or clients.
- Add up the revenue by practice groups and divide by the number of clients. This average is a proxy for the cumulative revenue by client in a practice group.

- If you have flat fees, you can use those amounts for revenue from the new clients, even if there is additional add-on work. Over time, you can see how many additional matters result per fixed-fee client.

New clients and new matters for existing clients—Clients who have never been your clients or clients of your firm should be counted as the client is onboarded into the practice management system or added to your accounting system if you do not have a practice management system in place. Count each new client only once, even if they end up with multiple matters.

If you want to run a separate calculation for new matters to existing clients, you can create a second KPI that measures the time spent upselling using the same calculation. However, investing time doing this calculation is worth the effort if upselling is a large percentage of your new matters and you believe that there is a disproportionate amount of time spent on existing client development.

§ 5:4 Background

Business development is hard, and not all lawyers are good at generating revenue. In a firm that has more than one person doing business development, the CAC KPI can be analyzed by attorney to see if there are any material differences between the results. Perhaps one attorney will be better off servicing clients rather than spending valuable billable time developing new business.

Nevertheless, how much did it cost to acquire that new client in the first place? This is often difficult to answer with any certainty because most firms' time and billing systems are not set up to gather the information needed. For example, how much time was spent with a client before they became a client? And when new clients come on, how much revenue will they generate?

Clients are demanding predictability, so even if your firm is not interested in offering flat fees, the client will want to know how much they will be spending. An added benefit of calculating CAC and CLV is this information can be used with other KPIs to establish pricing, whether that is billable hours or fixed fees.

Once you know that you spent less money acquiring your new clients than that potential revenue, you can look at the Productivity and Profitability KPIs to see what types of clients are most beneficial to the overall bottom line of the firm. Where is the biggest visible contribution? The KPIs are integrated, so metrics should be interpreted understanding the relationships and dependencies.

Our firm example is a solo and, therefore, a section discussing about how to adapt the CAC calculation for a slightly larger firm follows the firm example.

§ 5:5 Firm Example: CAC IP

CAC IP is a solo intellectual property boutique firm run by Charlie A. Copy. Charlie spent seven years as an associate in Big Law working with startups on their intellectual property registrations and licensing. He left early last spring and set up his own firm as a solo May 1, 2015.

As he heads into his second year, he decides to gather some metrics on how much it is costing him to secure new business. Charlie is also considering flat fees, and potentially subscriptions, for ongoing clients. His early-stage clients are somewhat price sensitive, so he is looking for cost-effective ways to leverage technology to attract and retain clients.

However, when Charlie works with companies that are passed the startup stage, raising a second round of financing, the projects expand beyond patent or trademark protection or licensing work, and he is sometimes bringing in other lawyers to assist. Often his clients look to Charlie as an outside counsel replacement, and as a result he ends up doing some basic business law also.

Charlie has a cloud-based practice management system that includes time and billing and also uses the Xero accounting system with some help from his virtual assistant, who also sets appointments. He uses a paid version of MailChimp to send out e-mails and keep track of the e-mails for his monthly newsletter. He does not have a formal customer relationship management system (CRM). He uses Microsoft Office 365, including Outlook. His website is very simple, with a "Contact Us" form and phone number that goes directly to his mobile phone.

Charlie does not rent an office but works out of a coworking space and books meeting rooms when he needs to meet with clients. He will use Excel to calculate the CAC information, as his practice management system does not capture all this information in one place.

Charlie's vision for his practice is to work hard but try to have time left over for some pro-bono and volunteer activities and a decent personal life, which includes taking time off in July and August. Ultimately he would like to make about $500,000 in billings per year and has set his billing rate at $250 per hour. Doing simple math and relying on the billable-hour model, Charlie will have to bill 2,000 hours in a year to reach his revenue target, which is why he is interested in exploring alternative fees.

In the fall of 2015, Charlie spent time at local and national events targeted at biomedical and Internet of things technology companies. He was both a presenter and an attendee. In conjunction with those events, Charlie started offering his potential clients a free IP review. On average that means Charlie spends at least one hour with the client and sometimes up to another hour preparing for that initial meeting.

His goal is to only spend $250 to secure a client because he can make that money back by billing one hour. Charlie has been researching the idea of having some of his clients pay a flat monthly fee or subscription, but he is so early stage that he does not have the information to create such a plan.

Costs

Charlie reviews his account listing and realizes that in 2015 he was putting all his travel in the same account, which includes his travel for conferences unrelated to business development, like the international IP conference, which was overseas, and the other American Bar Association meetings, for which he is very active.

Action: Luckily, he is able to send his virtual assistant a note, and the data entry is amended to have the travel allocated properly for Jan 2016 and forward.

All of Charlie's client costs are in these two accounts:
- Advertising—amounts spent on Google ads, sponsoring lunches and events at local accelerators.
- Sales & Marketing—MailChimp software costs, travel and conference registrations for business development, collateral for the office, website development costs, and client lunches.

Revenue and New Clients

Charlie implemented his accounting system the first day of his practice, but he did not set up his firm on the legal practice management (LPM) system until later in the summer. As he was very busy, he used the system for the any clients that he was doing billable working for on August 1st. Therefore, CAC IP has a gap in client revenue history in the LPM from May to the end of July.

Action: Charlie pays his assistant to update all the client information in the LPM to match the accounting records for revenue and all the time and billing information as well as the new clients and matters.

Timekeeping

Charlie tracks billable hours only by client. He does not track any client development or professional development time, nor any administrative time. In the first three months of the CAC IP, Charlie used the accounting system to send out the bills and used Excel to track his time for these billings. Therefore, the LPM is missing nonbillable time information for all of 2015 and for a three-month period for the billable work last May to August.

The time that it would take to go back through the eight months of calendars and notes for try to recreate the nonbillable time would exceed the benefits of potentially inaccurate information.

Action: Charlie pays his assistant to enter the missing billable time for the three-month period. Charlie creates three nonbillable time codes, one for client development, one for professional development, and one for general administration, and starts tracking that time in 2016.

Targets

Charlie has set CAC IP overall revenue target at $500,000 and thinks his average client will provide an annual value of about $5,000, so he needs 100 clients of that size per year. He would like to move towards a flat fee and keep his clients year after year on more of a subscription basis, but he thinks it is more realistic to look at the cumulative lifetime value of a client as their startup amount, which may take place over about six months and ranges between $2,500 and $7,500 per client. Finally, as stated, he wants to have a target CAC of $250 per client.

Action: Charlie keeps his target at $250 and will track all revenue by client for pricing and lifetime value.

§ 5:6 Firm example: CAC IP—First quarter results

Charlie has been reviewing CAC(a) Client Acquisition Cost and CAC(b) Upsell Rate each month. Although the other two KPIs are only annual, Charlie did some early calculations because CAC and Upsell were performing poorly.

Overall, Charlie was shocked at the results. He thought he was actually spending much less time this year on new client acquisition than last year.

Deep Dive KPI 2: Cost of Client Acquisition (CAC) § 5:6

2-CAC (a): Client Acquisition Cost (CAC) for the first quarter in 2016:

CAC IP 2016			
	Jan	Feb	Mar
2-CAC(a) Client Acquisition Cost ($)	$2,950	$1,750	$1,080
TARGET -Client Acquisition Cost ($)	$250	$250	$250
Input—advertising, sales & marketing costs	$450	$1,500	$240
Billable hour value in client development*	$2,500	$2,000	$3,000
Input—number of billable hours in client development	10	8	12
Input—average billing rate for client development	$250	$250	$250
Total new clients (can instead link to the Client Development (CD) KPI info)	1	2	3

(note this can also be linked to the PERFORMANCE tab and adjusted to calculate billable hour value by individual timekeeper)

As CAC IP only has one timekeeper, the CAC is for Charlie only. In January, CAC was more than 10 times the target amount. The client that signed on for a new matter in January only needed some trademark work done, which was a total of $2,500. Charlie had spent more acquiring that client than the revenue it would generate!

Charlie had not spoken at any events in January but had set up four meetings with potential clients. At the end of the month he had spent 10 hours on those four clients and only won one new client.

Charlie had reviewed these results in early February and realized that when he was giving away an hour of time to potential clients, he was actually giving away closer to two and a half hours. Also, when he set the target at $250, he was not valuing his time at his billing rate but at his draw or salary rate, which was less than half that amount.

In February, Charlie actually meet with 12 potential clients and landed two new clients. Prior to these meetings, he decided to scale back the free IP review to a free 30-minute consultation. He was then able to spend less time preparing and schedule more meetings with potential clients. It appears that the CAC is going in the right direction.

Charlie also spent some money on his website in February to add in a dropdown menu with the different types of services and some questions to help him prepare for any meetings. He is determined to increase the number of potential leads per month and reduce the CAC to his target of $250 per client.

2-CAC (b): Upsell Rate for the first quarter in 2016:

CAC IP 2016			
	Jan	Feb	Mar
2-CAC(b) Upsell Rate (%)	NA	NA	0%
TARGET—Upsell Rate (%)	NA	NA	20%
Input—new matters from existing clients	0	0	0
Input total new matters	1	2	3

This is an area where Charlie sees that he needs more information and some techniques and perhaps tools. All of his new work in the first three months of 2016 was from new clients, but as his CAC calculations are demonstrating, this is expensive and time-consuming.

Charlie met with his mentor, who is now in-house counsel at a large local technology company. They discussed how creating an ongoing relationship with his medium-sized clients might be an avenue to grow the revenue with existing clients. For smaller clients, some regular check-in or providing information to spot legal issues was discussed.

**2-CAC (c): Client Lifetime or Annual Value (CLV) and
2-CAC (d): CLV to CAC Ratio**:

These two KPIs are set to be annual measurements, but Charlie ran some early numbers because he was concerned by his CAC and Upsell Rate results.

Based on his quick calculation from his LPM, the average client annual value (CLV) was about $4,000 per matter in the first three months of 2016. He checked, and most of the work he was doing was "one and done," or in other words, he signed up a new client for a new matter and when he was done, he was not winning any more work from that client. The duration of those matters were often less than six weeks. The average was skewed because he did win a patent filing that was close to $20,000 that was reflected in revenue in the first quarter.

When Charlie compared this $4,000 CLV to the March CAC of approximately $1,000, the ratio was four. In other words, every dollar spent on acquiring a client generates $4 of revenue. What does that mean? It means if it costs more than $3 to deliver the services, Charlie will start losing money. However, like the other KPIs, this 2-CAC(d) CLV to CAC Ratio calculation is just one piece of the entire puzzle.

Charlie had set a target of 20 for the CLV to CAC Ratio because his target CLV was $5,000 and his CAC was $250. Charlie decided to spend the remainder of 2016 focusing on upselling to existing clients, which would be less expensive than new prospective clients and also increase his cumulative lifetime revenue from clients.

§ 5:7 Firm example: CAC IP—Full year results

Exhibit 1 at the end of the chapter contains the full year results for the CAC IP client acquisition cost KPIs. Charlie's first quarter changes had a positive impact on all of the metrics. However, as the metrics show, Charlie did not take any time off over the summer and still fell short of his annual revenue target.

The CAC remained under $1,000 for the remainder of the year, and in November it dropped to $122, which is below the $250 target. When the numbers were run for the entire year, overall CAC was $486 for the 58 new clients. Although that is almost double the target, it is a significant improvement over the results early in the year. On average Charlie spent more than one hour per new client in the development process.

CAC IP 2016	
	ANNUAL
2-CAC(a) Client Acquisition Cost ($)	$486
TARGET Client Acquisition Cost ($)	$250
Total—advertising, sales & marketing costs	$10,940
Billable hour value in client development*	$17,250
Total—number of billable hours in client development	69
Total—average billing rate for client development	$250
Total new clients	58

Charlie was on and off as far as winning work from existing clients over the year. The Upsell Rate fluctuated from 0% to 24% and then down to 13%, finishing the year at 25%. Charlie tried to upsell his services as an outside in-house counsel and also received some follow-on patent work from some clients. He did not implement fixed fees, nor did he have a chance to use a subscription approach with any client. He did experiment with some flat fees for a couple of projects and had mixed responses from clients. Charlie is now implementing a client feedback survey and asking some questions around fees and satisfaction before formalizing any more changes.

The CLV and CLV to CAC Ratio were both under target. However, the CLV did increase from $4,000 at the end of the first quarter to $4,758 for the year. Given that overall revenue was less than budget, Charlie needs to review his pricing and dig deeper into the best mix of clients.

The CLV to CAC Ratio was 9.8, which was just short of half of the target of 20. However, a 9.8 ratio is excellent for a solo, as there are not many costs of delivering the service, particularly because Charlie does not even have an office. Charlie will revisit his pricing but should also consider reducing his target of 20.

Client Acquisition Process Changes

In the third quarter of the year, Charlie invested in software to automate more than half of his client interview questions and joined a paid referral network for his patent and trademark work. The sales and marketing costs associated with those projects were in the numbers for July through October and drove up those month's CAC. However, because the referrals were qualified clients that needed IP help, Charlie did not need to meet with all of them to do a free IP review. Instead, Charlie was able to have them use the software to provide all the information he normally spent almost an hour gathering in person. In the month of November, he secured nine new clients and only spent a total of four hours with the 12 prospective clients.

Pricing

The 2-CAC(c) Client Lifetime or Annual Value KPI provides good pricing data for flat or fixed fees calculations. Charlie can run a list of the cumulative revenue from his 72 clients in 2016 in addition to the 35 from 2015. Next, he can group them by type of matter and range of fees charged and collected. Charlie's first pass, after discarding the outliers, where he heavily discounted work in his first month, gives him the draft categories and ranges as follows:

Startup IP Review	$1,500 to $4,500
Trademark	$550 to $1,750
Patents	$10,000 to $27,500
Outside In-house IP Counsel	$12,500 to $15,000
IP Strategy & Licensing Projects	$2,000 to $12,500

Since he was contemplating subscription fees, Charlie will continue to monitor the Startup IP Review and Outside In-house IP Counsel numbers. It is not as simple as dividing the average by 12 months to create a monthly fee because Charlie would have to ensure that he was not providing all the work up front and running the risk of the client discontinuing the subscription before enough revenue had been received.

Pricing models start with this cumulative revenue data, but it is not a complete picture because it is important to also look internally at the productivity and profitability information and externally to competitors' rates.

Exhibit 1—Client Acquisition Cost (CAC) CAC IP 2016

CLIENT ACQUISITION COST (CAC)													
CAC IP 2016	Jan	Feb	Mar	Apr	May	June	July	Aug	Sept	Oct	Nov	Dec
2-CAC(a) Client Acquisition Cost ($)	$ 2,950	$ 1,750	$ 1,080	$ 625	$ 338	$ 350	$ 281	$ 275	$ 817	$ 536	$ 122	$ 300
TARGET -Client Acquisition Cost ($)	$ 250	$ 250	$ 250	$ 250	$ 250	$ 250	$ 250	$ 250	$ 250	$ 250	$ 250	$ 250
Input - advertising, sales & marketing costs	450	1500	240	1000	100	750	1500	1500	1200	2500	100	100
Billable hour value in client development*	2500	2000	3000	1500	1250	1000	750	1250	1250	1250	1000	500
Input - number of billable hours in client dev.	10	8	12	6	5	4	3	5	5	5	4	2
Input - Average billing rate Client Development	$250	$250	$250	$250	$250	$250	$250	$250	$250	$250	$250	$250
Total new clients (can instead link to the Client Development (CD) KPI info)	1	2	3	4	4	5	8	10	3	7	9	2

(*note this can also be linked to the PERFORMANCE tab and adjusted to calculate Billable hour value by individual timekeeper)

CAC IP 2016	Jan	Feb	Mar	Apr	May	June	July	Aug	Sept	Oct	Nov	Dec
2-CAC(b) Upsell Rate (%)			0%			24%			13%			25%
TARGET - Upsell Rate (%)			20%			20%			20%			20%
Input - new matters from existing clients	0	0	0	2	1	1	3	0	0	3	3	0
Input total new matters	1	2	3	6	5	6	11	10	3	10	12	2

CAC IP 2016	Jan	Feb	Mar	Apr	May	June	July	Aug	Sept	Oct	Nov	Dec
2-CAC(c)Client Life-time or Annual Value - CLV ($)												$ 4,758
TARGET -Client Life-time or Annual Value - CLV ($)												$ 5,000
Input - cumulative revenue												$342,600
Input - total clients served												72

CAC IP 2016	Jan	Feb	Mar	Apr	May	June	July	Aug	Sept	Oct	Nov	Dec
2-CAC(d) - CLV to CAC Ratio (#)												9.8
TARGET -Life-time or Annual client value - CV or LTV ($) Ratio to CAC												20
Input - average life time billing by client**												$ 4,758
Monthly CAC - average over the year (from 2-CAC(a))												$ 486

(**note this can be refined to be a monthly average or by type of client and more than one calculation created)

§ 5:8 Firm example: CAC IP—Prior year data points

CAC IP only has eight months of data for 2015. On the cost side, Charlie made the decision that it is not worth his time to go back to review all the costs in these accounts in 2015 to make corrections because he was in startup mode in the first eight months of the firm. He feels that he spent an extraordinary amount of money on early advertising and promotion, so trying to calculate CAC for 2015 new clients would not be useful because it is skewed.

However, as outlined above, Charlie ensured that the 2015 data was cleaned up for revenue and billable hours, and that allowed Charlie to run CLV for 2015. The average of $5,486 is above his target of $5,000, but he fell short of that in 2016. Charlie's changes to his pricing and offerings mean that his target should change or he should consider doing calculations by client type instead of firm-wide.

CAC IP PART YEAR 2015	
2-CAC(c)Client Lifetime or Annual Value—CLV ($)	$5,486
TARGET -Client Lifetime or Annual Value—CLV ($)	$5,000
Input—cumulative revenue	$192,000
Input—total clients served	35

§ 5:9 Technology to assist with client acquisition cost KPIs

Properly implemented technology can not only assist with data collection and reduce duplication of tasks, but also improve and streamline law firm workflow or process. Some of the technology that can be used to assist with Client Acquisition Cost KPIs:

- Excel—To avoid problems with various versions of the same spreadsheet, users should use a safe shared drive or server and create links between different workbooks and sheets to simplify data input.
- Accounting Software—As accounting for legal services is more complex than the average small business, an accounting system that handles trust accounting and modified accrual may be necessary.

- Legal Practice Management (LPM)—The number of new clients and new matters should be generated from the LPM, and revenue by client for any period should be available but may require a custom report.
- Time and Billing Software—Again, due to the billing complexities and modified accounting methods, time and billing software that is separate from the accounting or LPM system may be necessary. However, the LPM, accounting system, and time & billing must integrate.
- Customer Relationship Management (CRM)—A pipeline and the number of calls or interviews can usually be created within a CRM, and the clients' information can be shared on an ongoing basis.
- Appointment Setting—Software programs or virtual assistants can help with setting meetings with prospective clients.
- Calendar—Many LPMs and calendars can integrate and synchronize to share data on appointments and follow-up tasks.
- Interview automation software—Depending on the area of the law, there are various companies who have designed software that collects information from prospective clients on the firm website, thus saving time.
- Document automation and registration—There are various software programs that automate standard document assembly or gather the info for registration of IP, such as trademarks or patents. When attorneys use these systems, they can automate the tasks that do not require any professional judgment and allow for efficiencies.

A nonexhaustive list of technology resources is in APPENDIX D.

§ 5:10 Common mistakes or pitfalls

The above firm example and other experiences give rise to lessons learned that are set out below as common mistakes or pitfalls to avoid:

- Charts of Accounts are not useful. Accounting is a necessary evil in the eyes of many, but the information is powerful if firms have a good understanding of the various accounts and if they are diligent about recording the information properly. If the accounts are set up only to record historical information and without thinking about how these accounts feed the numbers into the KPIs, the KPIs will not be as useful.

- "Garbage in—Garbage out" holds true. This is an old systems consulting adage that applies anytime you are making a decision to record revenue, costs, or time. Have a clear understanding of what goes into which account and be consistent.
- Accounting of nonbillable time can be too detailed. Remember that the nonbillable time is averaged over the new clients that are acquired. If you spend too much time worrying about dividing up your non-billable pursuit time to all the potential clients, you are not refining your measurement. Keep things at a high level until you see an issue and at that point, you can dive deeper into the problem area.
- The Client Lifetime Value can be overanalyzed. The Client Lifetime Value metric is an area where it is more of an art to figure out how deep to dive into the measurements as outlined above in pricing. Starting with firm results and then digging deeper into the various types of clients and in some cases, all the way down to the individual clients may be necessary. However, start at the aggregate, following the KISS principle, and see first where the problem areas lie for your firm.
- Comparing apples to oranges can occur. The KPI 2-CAC(d) CLV to CAC Ratio can be calculated at various levels of detail, and sometimes the numbers can be mixed up, which can lead to false reporting and actions. For example, if you have several different types of clients and you are calculating CAC based on one client or client type and you are comparing that to the firm CLV, the results can be skewed.

§ 5:11 Small firms

The above CAC KPIs can be used for one, two, or even three timekeepers who are doing the client development work. However, once you have multiple attorneys developing client business, you may wish to adjust the 2-CAC(a) Client Acquisition Cost to build up differently and have the cost results by client rather than an average for the firm. Calculating by practice area is also an option.

The client development direct and indirect costs are built up by attorney, instead of firm- wide, costs. In the larger of the small firms, each attorney may have their own sales and marketing budget and can track their client development time. The same calculation can be used, but instead of firm-wide costs, use the attorney's costs plus an allocation from any firm-wide costs. That allocation would be calculated the same way as above. Therefore, the 2 CAC(a) calculation has an added component, bolded below:

§ 5:11

Advertising, sales, and marketing spend by attorney, **plus advertising, sales, and marketing spend—firm allocation,** plus opportunity cost of the lawyer and staff time divided by the number of new clients for that lawyer.

Below is the revised Attorney CAC calculation which would then be compared to the CLV for that attorney's clients.

CAC for SMALL LAW (ATTORNEY)	
	Jan
2-CAC(a) Client Acquisition Cost ($)	**$588**
TARGET Client Acquisition Cost ($)	$500
Input—FIRM—advertising, sales & marketing costs	$375
Input—advertising, sales & marketing costs	$100
ATTORNEY Billable-hour value in client development*	$700
Input—number of billable hours in client development	2
Input—ATTORNEY billing rate for client development	$350
Total new clients (can instead link to the Client Development (CD) KPI info)	2

* *(Billable hour value by individual timekeeper)*

The above shows that the Attorney CAC is $588 against a target of $500. The $588 breaks down as follows:
   Attorney time—$350
   Attorney advertising, sales & marketing—$50
   Firm advertising, sales & marketing—$188

Without the firm allocation of $188, the attorney would have achieved her target CAC. However, that firm allocation likely allows the attorney to attract potential clients and is part of the support received from a small firm.

For firms that approach the 30-lawyer mark and have department-wide client pursuits, the ideal is to calculate CAC by client. First, track the development hours by client rather than lumping the hours together and taking an average of the new clients. It may also make sense to track the time associated with each of the pursuits and then again apply the individual rates to create the billable hour value for all the attorneys on the pursuit. The following is an example of the CAC for a single client pursuit.

CAC SMALL LAW (FIRM)	
	CLIENT XYZ
2-CAC(a) Client Acquisition Cost ($)	**$5,175**
TARGET -Client Acquisition Cost ($)	$5,000
Input—FIRM—advertising, sales & marketing costs	$375
Input—CLIENT- advertising, sales & marketing costs	$1,500
**ATTORNEYS	ADMIN billable-hour value in client development***	$3,300
Input—number of billable hours in client development	12
Input—ATTORNEY billing rate for client development	Various

Remember the metrics need to match your workflow and size of firm. Adjust your approach where necessary to receive the best results.

In the next chapter, we look at a mix of traditional and client-centric measures around the third KPI—Profitability—this time with a small commercial litigation firm.

Chapter 6

Deep Dive KPI 3: Productivity (PROD)

§ 6:1　Introduction
§ 6:2　KPI 3—Productivity (PROD) summary
§ 6:3　Data and sources
§ 6:4　Background
§ 6:5　Firm example: PRODUCT LIT
§ 6:6　—First quarter results
§ 6:7　—Full year results
§ 6:8　—Prior year data points
§ 6:9　Technology to assist with productivity KPIs
§ 6:10　Common mistakes or pitfalls

§ 6:1 Introduction

After the new client work is won, we need to measure the delivery efficiency or the team's productivity. The productivity KPIs do not include traditional utilization metrics. In fact, we do not measure billable hours by individual attorney or other timekeeper in the usual fashion within the KPIs.

Overall, it is directly relevant to firm profitability to measure collections rather than billings. How much time is spent on a project is important for calculating costs, pricing, and profitability, but not necessarily a standalone measure of efficiency or effective use of resources.

Therefore, with productivity we will look at billable hours on the aggregate for the number of attorneys and paralegals, but on the individual level, we will look to revenue and collections for performance measures.

A quick note on the impact of alternative fee arrangements and recording hours: Regardless of fee structure, the metrics are the same for profitability and productivity, we are laser focused on cash collection. Alternative fee arrangements are important for survival in a very competitive market but will not alter your KPI implementation. It is important though to collect information on nonbillable time. Some firms have moved away from recording these nonbillable hours. I am not suggesting an onerous nonbillable system, but in order to evaluate the time spent acquiring clients, business or client development time needs to be captured.

§ 6:1   LAW FIRM KEY PERFORMANCE INDICATORS

Remember that nonbillable hours are a lost opportunity for generating revenue, and understanding where all the hours go is critically important.

§ 6:2 KPI 3—Productivity (PROD) summary

The third KPI area of Productivity (PROD) contains seven metrics as outlined in the table below, and APPENDIX B, Comprehensive KPI Listing—KPI 3: Productivity, presents the information in table format with formulas.

3-PROD Metrics	Calculation	Frequency**
3-PROD (a): Client Pipeline (#)	Number of active clients divided by the total attorneys (and paralegals* if they work directly for clients)	Monthly
3-PROD (b): Revenue per Matter ($)	Total revenue for the period divided by the number of open matters	Monthly
3-PROD (c): Rent Expense (%)	Total rent expense divided by the total revenue on the financial statements	Quarterly
3-PROD (d): Attorney Leverage (%)	Total dollar value of the all attorney billings divided by the total billings	Quarterly
3-PROD (e): Paralegal Leverage (%)	Total dollar value of the all paralegal billings divided by the total billings	Quarterly
3-PROD (f): Attorneys' Productivity (%)	Total number of hours billed by all attorneys divided by hours available to bill for the same attorneys	Annually
3-PROD (g): Paralegals' Productivity (%)	Total dollar value of the all paralegal billings divided by the total billings	Annually

*This is a point worth expanding upon. If the paralegals are supporting the attorneys and not generating their own work, you would not include the number of paralegals into the calculation. However, you need to always compare like calculations. More on this below in the firm example.

DEEP DIVE KPI 3: PRODUCTIVITY (PROD) § 6:3

** We recommend that KPIs should be tracked regularly, either monthly, quarterly, or annually once fully implemented. In the early stages of adoption, try to collect as much data as possible monthly and do an assessment at the end of the first quarter, including a comparison to the prior year. Some metrics will lend themselves to monthly measurement, while others will be naturally quarterly or annually. However, each firm's situation will be different, and there is simply no right or wrong approach to measurement; therefore, the frequencies listed in the table are only recommendations or examples.

§ 6:3 Data and sources

Productivity KPI data comes mainly from the time and billing systems. Those functions are usually handled by the accounting system, legal practice management (LPM) system, or a combination of both. The rent expense will come from the monthly financial reports produced by the accounting system.

Active Clients—Consistency for comparisons is important when pulling data for KPIs. Active clients are not only new clients nor old clients. Active clients are considered those clients where there was time spent on the matter during the month, other than administrative tasks like issuing an invoice.

Billings—Come from the practice management system, time and billing, or the accounting system, depending on your billing process and software. Here the concept of matching is important, regardless of the whether you are measuring for a month, quarter, or year. The billings for the period should match with the effort for the same period to calculate productivity.

Therefore, even if you use cash basis for recognizing revenue, using the billings number will achieve matching of the effort with revenue. However, if you are recording time for one month but not sending out bills until the next month, you may have a matching issue when calculating productivity because your billings have a month time lag. The time and effort should be matched with the billable amount created, and in that case, you may wish to use unbilled time or work in progress (WIP) as a proxy for billings when calculating productivity measures. In the end, understanding the data for your measurements allows you to see if it makes a difference to adjust any of the inputs for timing.

Revenue—Billings are not necessarily equal to revenue: It depends on the accounting method for revenue recognition. There is no right or wrong method; it is just important to define when you are recognizing revenue for your firm and gather the data to see if there any large fluctuations that may require adjustments to the KPI formulas. We have built these challenges into our firm example.

Revenue is recognized for hours recorded at one of three points in time below:

Unbilled Time (WIP) = Revenue for Accrual Method

In the Accrual Method, revenue is recognized as soon as the time is recorded and the hours become Unbilled Time or WIP. Usually the WIP is reviewed to ensure that it is all billable and ultimately collectible. If flat or fixed fees are used, revenue can be recognized based on a progress basis.

If revenue is recognized when WIP is created, there does not have to be a billing to create revenue. In other words, when the WIP is actually billed to the client, the accounts receivable (A/R) is created, but the revenue has already been created.

This method matches the effort with the revenue directly in the same period, but billings are not equal to revenue under this method.

Billed Time (A/R) = Revenue for Modified Accrual Method

In contrast, in the Modified Accrual Method, revenue is not recognized when time is recorded into Unbilled Time or WIP. Rather, it is recognized once the WIP is billed to the client. This recognition is one step later than the accrual method.

The amount comes from WIP into A/R and then revenue is recognized. Therefore, revenue may occur the same month if WIP is billed the same month, but may lag by a month or even two if the billings are one or two months later.

If clients have paid a retainer, the money would be drawn down from the retainer account to pay the A/R, but the revenue is based on issuing the bill. In this case, billings are equal to revenue.

Collected Time (Cash) = Revenue for Cash Method

In the Cash Method, revenue is recognized once the cash is collected. Cash can come from a billing or A/R; a flat fee without a retainer arrangement; or payment from a client retainer in a trust account.

In this case, the cash received does not match the effort that month, and therefore, productivity measures may need to be adjusted for revenue when you are doing month by month. If it is over a year, the spikes in cash collection can be somewhat smoothed out. Again, it is always a good idea to check the results for prior year.

Revenue from Financial Statements—The three methods referenced above include revenue for all firm matters. The firm may have additional revenue in terms of interest on late payments or pass-through revenue which is for cocounsel or specialists. The latter is something that will be on the financial statements but should not be mixed into the revenue per matter, as it will skew the results for productivity and profitability. For example, if the monthly billing was $25,000, and that included an expert witness of $10,000, then if you compare the revenue of $25,000 to the hours billed within the firm, it will then misstate the results. The expert witness amount does not have any internal hours associated with the $10,000, so it needs to be removed from the Revenue per Matter but will be included in the revenue on the financial statements but the cost or pass thru amount of $10,000 will be in the cost section. More is included on this concept under the profitability KPI section.

A final note is that none of these three types of time are the same as *billable* hours. It is best to think of billable hours as aspirational because those hours may not even qualify as unbilled time.

Flat Fees and Cash Method

Flat fees can be complicated for productivity and profitability KPIs if you are using the cash method because the fee may be paid up front or on a monthly basis. The payments will not necessarily match to the effort and the costs of the work with the revenue.

Sometimes, if you gather your data, the cash received can be a good approximation for the revenue over a longer period of time. However, profitability KPIs and pricing rely on good data. Particularly, time and progress information are fundamental for pricing.

Pricing

As flat or fixed fees become more popular for legal services, we can look to the engineering profession for a revenue recognition, productivity, and profitability measurement approach. Although the earned value method is complex for simple legal services, the concepts can be borrowed and simplified. We will use a single criminal defense case to illustrate the earned-value method.

Joe engages Jack, a lawyer, for a $10,000 flat fee. Jack charges the fee up front, and it is not a retainer. Joe's case is for a criminal defense. Jack estimates that Joe's case will last six months, including a trial that is one day and maximum of six pretrial hearings if it goes ahead. Joe makes a list of these milestones and assigns estimates of hours and calculates progress based on the hours.

Month 1:

Milestone	Estimate of Hours
Court Appearance	1.5 hours
Initial Research | Letter	3 hours
Pretrial Hearing	1.5 hour
Total hours	6 hours, or 15% of the full case.

Total estimated hours were 40; therefore, based on hours, after the first month you will be 15% complete. The 40 hours comes from data for work on past, similar cases, and Jack tries to recover about $250 per hour for the case.

After the first month, Jack appeared in court once and had one pretrial hearing and some research, in addition to authoring a letter requesting a deviation, so he achieved his milestones. However, when Jack looks at the time keeping, he has recorded 12 hours because the research was 7.5 hours instead of 3, and he had two lengthy meetings with Joe that were not included in his budget. According to the milestones, Jack is 15% done, but when you look at the hours, Jack used up 30% of the time budget.

If Jack was recognizing revenue solely based on effort, in this case the hours recorded, he would recognize $3,000. However, based on progress on the milestones, he really should only recognize $1,500 of revenue for the month because he is only 15% complete.

From a productivity standpoint, Jack is working at a 50% productivity rate. For every hour Jack is spending on the case, he is only earning half an hour in terms of revenue. Once this occurs, you cannot go back and change the budget, but you can use this information for budgeting and pricing in the future cases.

Looking forward a couple of months after Joe's case settles with a plea, you may have a windfall in terms of revenue recognition because you may finish the case and be able to recognize the remainder of the $10,000 without recording any additional time. Productivity will be positively impacted because you are able to recognize revenue without resources. By gathering these statistics, Jack has invaluable data for pricing future cases. This earned-value approach is transferable to any time of law where you have a repeatable process to establish milestones and budgeted time or effort.

§ 6:4 Background

Productivity is not to be confused with being busy. Often professionals, not just attorneys, think that billing hours is being productive. Lawyers are given billable hour targets, and often they do not think through the impact of billing too many hours or not recording all of their time. They are laser focused on achieving targets. Therefore, partners have to align their firm productivity and profitability targets with the individual goals.

Looking at the profession as a whole, there is a shift to flat fees and even subscription, but that will not mean that hours should no longer be recorded. As the example above demonstrates, the hours are valuable data for pricing and productivity.

Shifting away from measuring the input or the supply of hours is a fundamental change. In some ways, the legal profession is stuck in the industrial revolution, where the answer was to add labor to solve a problem. This is also seen in the reluctance to adopt technology. Technology can add another wrinkle because lawyers do not want to replace potential billable hours with a software solution. There is this notion that they need to keep their billable hours up regardless of what is best for the client. Efficiency is desired by the client, but if your associates are measured by whether they hit a billable hour target, the objectives conflict.

Also, there can be a problem when associates or paralegals are given a budget for billable hours and they then do not wish to exceed the budget, so they only record the hours to keep within the budget. Unfortunately, long term that will hurt the practice because the billing rates and any flat-fee pricing is based on the historical time to complete tasks. Perhaps the pricing was not enough and as a result the budgeted hours were too low. Therefore, if the true actual hours are not recorded, the pricing and budget will never be adjusted. Likewise, if the associate or paralegal is taking too long to complete a task, perhaps he or she was not assigned to the right type of work or needs additional training on the task.

§ 6:5 Firm example: PRODUCT LIT

PRODUCT LIT is a commercial litigation firm started five years ago by three former law school friends after they all worked at local mid-sized firms. The three partners offer business and commercial litigation trial and appellate work in addition to construction and real estate litigation. One of the partners, Philip Light, will take on product liability cases and insurance defense litigation. Another partner, Patty Leigh, offers mediation in partnership with an outside firm.

The firm uses an outside bookkeeping service and works on the modified accrual basis. The bookkeeper visits the firm once a month to run all the bills on the 27th, or the closest working day to the 27th, of each month. The time and billing is done through a cloud-based practice management system, and QuickBooks online is used for accounting. At this point, the fee structure is the traditional billable hour based on approved billing rates. The firm does not bill separately for office disbursements: the billing rates are to include copies, postage, and the like.

The firm's revenue target was $2.5 million in 2015, but they did not hit that number, falling short by approximately $600,000. Their clients seem happy with the results, but recently several have moved their appeals to other firms. Penelope Law lobbied her other two partners to hire two paralegals because the two associate attorneys were overwhelmed and the firm had had to outsource some work at a high hourly rate to complete some matters last fall.

The firm promises every client that one of the three partners will be involved in their case. Penelope does not think that the partners are making appropriate use of the two associates in terms of assigning the right work to them and that there is enough work to keep the new paralegals busy. Also, the administrative assistant has extensive training, having been with the firm since the beginning. Penelope believes that the firm productivity could be improved by looking at KPIs and reassigning work.

When the three partners sit down to discuss productivity KPIs in the first week of January 2016, Philip brings up his concern that, although the two attorneys seemed overwhelmed last fall, their billable hours were lower than target. Penelope explains that the hours that are recorded are not necessarily the amount of time spent on the files, as the associates were given budgets for each matter and strict instructions to stay on budget. More and more of their clients are asking for fixed fees for litigation, and as a compromise, both Philip and Patty have taken on some new cases that are still billable hours but overall cannot exceed a certain amount without first gaining client approval. Patty has a new breach of contract case where she has promised the client that the fee from PRODUCT LIT directly for work through trial will not exceed $60,000. Other, similar cases that have gone to trial, and the billings were closer to $80,000. Patty is confident that they can use the paralegal and associate for much of the research, whereas in the previous cases, she did the research herself.

Action: The partners agree that they should first look at the firm productivity and leverage before diving into the individual performance KPIs. Perhaps the partners have set the associates up for failure in terms of the traditional utilization targets. With the new paralegal starting this same first week of January, the partners agree to suspend the personal targets and focus on the best use of resources for the client.

The billing rates have been reviewed for 2016, and the three partners bill at the same rate, $300 per hour, with the associates at $150. It is decided that the paralegals will bill at $100 per hour and that the administrative assistant will not bill her hours.

Targets

The KPI targets are all just aspirational estimates for the first three months, other than the rent expense, because with the new hires and the new focus on leverage, last year's results were not particularly helpful

Action: The three partners agree to keep the same $2.5 million revenue target for 2016. Since it is the first time gathering data other than individual billable hours, the partners ask the bookkeeper and administrative assistant to create an Excel workbook and gather the data monthly for all the productivity KPIs in the first quarter.

§ 6:6 Firm example: PRODUCT LIT—First quarter results

The partners meet in the first week of February and the first week of each month afterwards to review the data and see the results for each KPI. At the end of the three months some targets are adjusted, and they ask the bookkeeper and administrative assistant to provide as much 2015 data as possible.

3-PROD (a): Client Pipeline for the first three months of 2016:

PRODUCT LIT 2016			
	Jan	Feb	Mar
3-PROD(a) Client Pipeline (#)	14	13	14
TARGET—Client Pipeline (#)	10	10	10
Input—total number of active firm clients	72	66	70
Input—total attorneys	5	5	5

Client pipeline is a new concept to PRODUCT LIT because they have never measured or set a target number of active clients per attorney. In 2016 the goal is to involve the attorneys in the cases with the partners in a more active way; therefore, the clients are to be shared amongst the five practicing attorneys. The three partners will be named to each of the cases, but the associates, both of whom have practiced for five years, are capable of running a case with limited assistance.

The results here worry the partners because an average of 14 cases per attorney means that there are about 28 cases between the two associates that need one of the three partners for assistance. That means that instead of 14 cases for each of the three partners, it is closer to 24 cases, depending on the type of law.

The target remains 10, but the partners ask the administrative assistant to flag the cases as small, medium, and large based on a range of billings as follows:

- Small, from $5,000 to $15,000
- Medium, from $15,000 to $30,000
- Large, above $30,000.

Once that information is gathered for 2016, the partners will review performance and the KPIs by size of billings to determine the right mix of cases.

Deep Dive KPI 3: Productivity (PROD) § 6:6

3-PROD (b): Revenue per Matter for the first three months:

PROD LIT 2016			
	Jan	Feb	Mar
3-PROD(b) Revenue per Matter ($)	$2,267	$2,794	$1,929
TARGET—Revenue per Matter ($)	$5,000	$5,000	$5,000
Input—total revenue for all matters	$170,000	$190,000	$135,000
Input—# open matters	75	68	70

PROD LIT recognizes the revenue when the unbilled time is billed under the modified accrual method. Therefore, the $170,000 of revenue recognized in January was moved from unbilled time or WIP that was created before January 27th. In theory, if all the WIP is billed out each month on the 27th, the January unbilled time would include efforts from the period December 27th to January 26th.

The question came up about the time from January 27th to the 31st, or this "stub period." Since a full month of time is included that is most of January, it is assumed that December 27th to 31st is basically the same amount of time, so you have the "month" of January as December 27th to January 26th. Also, you are matching the time recorded with the time billed within the same period, December 27th to January 26th.

When the target was set, the partners had used the smallest case size of $5,000 as an estimate. The actual results were much lower than $5K, but that was because most matters last much more than a month. The partners also forgot about some of the smaller cases that the attorneys were working on and underestimated the sheer number of active matters. The targets will be adjusted for the remainder of the year, and the partners will discuss their policy of being involved in every client matter, particularly the small client matters that are under $10,000 in total fees.

§ 6:6

3-PROD (c): Rent Expense for the first three months:

PRODUCT LIT 2016			
	Jan	Feb	Mar
3-PROD(c)Rent Expense (%)	3.1%	2.7%	4.8%
TARGET—Rent Expense (%)	3.0%	3.0%	3.0%
Input—rent expense	$5,500	$5,500	$7,500
Total Revenue per Financial Statements	$180,000	$205,000	$155,000

The two new paralegals started in January, but in March one more paralegal hire made additional office space necessary, and, therefore, the rent went up to $7,500 per month, and the partners had to sign a three-year lease. There is room for two more attorneys or four paralegals with the new space.

Philip used 3% of revenue as a target based on some research he did on law firm spending. The partners decided to continue measuring this each month for the remainder of the year to get a better baseline and also take a look at last year. Patty was interested in whether they could hire additional paralegals or attorneys that might share space and, therefore, generate more hours without a rental space commitment.

3-PROD (d): Attorney Leverage for the first three months:

PRODUCT LIT 2016			
	Jan	Feb	Mar
3-PROD(d) Attorney Leverage (%)	NA	NA	92%
TARGET—Attorney Leverage (%)	NA	NA	90%
Input total billings by all attorneys*	$150,000	$175,000	$130,000
Input total billings by firm	$170,000	$190,000	$135,000

(can be linked to "PERFORMANCE KPI" tab in any Excel workbook to avoid double entry of data)

When the partners reviewed the Attorney Leverage KPI after the first quarter, they were somewhat surprised by the results and quickly realized that they needed to dig a level deeper within this measure. The 92% leverage meant that the five attorneys, including the three partners, are doing 92% of the billable work.

Deep Dive KPI 3: Productivity (PROD) § 6:6

Patty is the rainmaker partner at this time and very concerned that the other partners are spending too much time on billable work and are not delegating enough work to the two nonpartner attorneys and paralegals. In larger firms, this type of calculation would have been the default. With a smaller firm, it is best to start at the highest level and split data differently because, at most small firms, there are not partners who just manage the business or just sell new work; it is usually high billing targets for the principals.

A second level of analysis is run to show the leverage for the two attorneys as nonpartners, and the three-month results overall were 29% of the billings for the first quarter; below are the calculations for the individual months for the two attorneys:

PRODUCT LIT 2016			
	Jan	Feb	Mar
3-PROD(d)(i) NONPARTNER Attorney Leverage (%)	26%	32%	31%
TARGET—NONPARTNER Attorney Leverage (%)	?	?	?
Input total billings by nonpartner attorneys	$43,500	$60,000	$41,250
Input total billings by firm	$170,000	$190,000	$135,000

This second level or 3-PROD(d)(i) Nonpartner Attorney Leverage gives some interesting information when presented with the 3-PROD (e) Paralegal Leverage (below) and the original 3-PROD(d) Attorney Leverage three-month figures.

First Quarter Leverage

Nonpartner Attorney   29%
Paralegal   8%
Partner Attorney   61%

The partners decide that the paralegal number is much too low and are pleased with the 61% figure for the partner billings until they realize that it is likely because the partner billing rate is $300 and the other attorneys are half that rate. However, when they discuss this with the bookkeeper, she points out that the other piece to the puzzle is aggregate billed hours.

Billable hours are actually just potential billable time and are not a measure of revenue. Billed hours are actually revenue once billed in PRODUCT LIT's situation. Please note that if flat fees are used, then the other piece of the puzzle is progress towards milestones, which is usually based on the recorded hours. The partners realize that setting targets for billable hours will not help with leverage; it is important to set budgets for the tasks and ensure that the tasks are delegated properly and all the hours are recorded.

3-PROD (e): Paralegal Leverage for the first three months:

PRODUCT LIT 2016			
	Jan	Feb	Mar
3-PROD(e) Paralegal Leverage (%)	NA	NA	8%
TARGET—Paralegal Leverage (%)	NA	NA	10%
Input total billings by all paralegals*	$20,000	$15,000	$5,000

* (can be linked to "PERFORMANCE KPI" tab in any Excel workbook to avoid double entry of data)

Penelope and Patty have taken on the management of the paralegals, particularly since Patty's $60,000 case needs a lot of up-front research and preparation. Patty initially had tried to outsource her research needs to contract attorneys but then realized that she was leaving the paralegals idle based on the 3-PROD(g) Paralegal Productivity KPIs of 63% in February. Penelope landed two new large cases in March, and, therefore, they both decided to hire another paralegal and closely track the work assignments to ensure that work flowed to now three paralegals.

3-PROD (f): Attorney Productivity for the first three months:

PRODUCT LIT 2016			
	Jan	Feb	Mar
3-PROD(f) Attorney Productivity (%)	78%	91%	68%
TARGET—Attorney Productivity (%)	80%	80%	80%
Input total #billed attorney hours	625	729	542
Input total #attorney	5	5	5
Input total hours available by firm	160	160	160

As outlined above, the leverage numbers showed that the attorneys were doing 92% of the billable work, but when the nonpartner attorneys were isolated, that number dropped to 61%. However, what did that mean in terms of the number of billed hours? Again, the measure is not billable but actual hours billed out within this month. Are the three partners productive or too productive?

The bookkeeper went back and split out the nonpartner attorney billed hours to create two KPIs: 3-PROD(f)(i) Nonpartner Attorney Productivity and also PROD(f)(ii) Partner Attorney Productivity.

PRODUCT LIT 2016			
	Jan	Feb	Mar
3-PROD(f)(i) NONPARTNER Attorney Productivity (%)	91%	125%	86%
TARGET—NONPARTNER Attorney Productivity (%)	?	?	?
Input total #billed nonpartner attorney hours	290	400	275
Input total # nonpartner attorneys	2	2	2
Input total hours available	160	160	160

PRODUCT LIT 2016			
	Jan	Feb	Mar
3-PROD(f)(ii) PARTNER Attorney Productivity (%)	70%	69%	56%
TARGET—PARTNER Attorney Productivity (%)	80%	80%	80%
Input total #billed attorney hours	335	329	267
Input total #attorneys	3	3	3
Input total hours available	160	160	160

By splitting the measure into two levels, the partners can see how work much is delegated from partners to associates in terms of effort; in PRODUCT LIT's situation, this is represented by hours. The results for the paralegals are below.

In February the productivity was as follows:

Partner Attorney	69%
Nonpartner Attorney	125%
Paralegal	63%

It seems like the work assignments are unequal. The partners meet in early March to discuss how the workload is unbalanced and how their goals for the remainder of the year should be to delegate more work to the paralegals. The two attorneys seem to be doing all the work and more based on the 125% productivity measure. Although it is great that they are generating billed hours that exceed targets, it is not a sustainable level of effort and may have a negative impact on the budget in terms of dollars. Based on these results, the partners sit down with the two attorneys and share the responsibility of delegating the work to the paralegals, asking that the attorneys do not go over 100% billed time.

Patty explains that if the attorneys do the work at $150 per hour instead of the paralegals at $100 per hour, the firm runs the risk of being over budget, and some of the attorney's billed time will not be able to be billed. One of the attorneys is concerned that the paralegals are not appropriately trained to do some of the tasks that are assigned to them in the budget. The partners meet and review the top 20 matters that involve paralegals and realize that they have budgeted based on the paralegals completing numerous tasks that the attorneys have been completing instead. Philip takes on training the paralegals, and the attorneys

Deep Dive KPI 3: Productivity (PROD) § 6:7

are assigned budget monitoring responsibility for all the small matters (those up to $15,000).

The partners also decide that once they properly train the paralegals that they will delegate more challenging work to the two other attorneys because they have the capacity.

3-PROD (g): Paralegal Productivity for the first three months:

PRODUCT LIT 2016			
	Jan	Feb	Mar
3-PROD(g) Paralegal Productivity (%)	83%	63%	14%
TARGET—Paralegal Productivity (%)	80%	80%	80%
Input total #billed paralegal hours	200	150	50
Input total #paralegals	2	2	3
Input total hours available	120	120	120

After the new paralegal hire and the pledge to keep the paralegals busy, the 14% in March is a difficult number to receive. However, most of the paralegal time in March was spent in training paralegals for the knowledge gap identified by the attorneys. In addition, the available hours were incorrect. Although the new paralegal started the first week of March, she spent two weeks shadowing another paralegal. Therefore, the available hours should have been adjusted. The bookkeeper has made a note to adjust available hours during the year for new hires, terminations, and vacations for more than a week.

§ 6:7 Firm example: PRODUCT LIT—Full year results

Exhibit 1 at the end of the chapter contains the full year results for the Productivity KPIs for PRODUCT LIT.

Overall the firm exceeded the $2.5 million revenue target for 2016, with total revenue of $2,695,000 that included billings of $2,530,000. The client pipeline shrank over the course of the year, but the makeup of the pipeline shifted from over 30 small cases to over 10 large cases. This change was evident as the revenue per matter per month also grew after the first quarter of the year, and by December, the target revenue per month was exceeded every month except one from May onwards. Upon further investigation, there were several large cases that settled in late October, so the billings and activity dropped temporarily in November.

For 2017, the pipeline will be divided into the three types of cases: small, medium, and large. The bookkeeper is going back through 2016 and 2015 to expand the data for the same three types of cases. The effort to find and classify cases is also to use the actual hours recorded and billed for pricing on a flat-fee basis. Patty's $60K case ended up at $75K, but the client was kept informed and happy with the experience. The milestone and actual information will allow Patty to better predict her next project where she must submit a fixed fee not to exceed a certain amount.

Rent expense was above the 3% target several times during the year; however, Philip decided that since the results for 2016 overall were an average of 3.3% and in 2015 with the rent at $66,000 and revenue at $1,865,000, the rent expense was actually higher at 3.5%, this is not an area where there needs to be concern as long as the revenue level continues.

After the paralegal retraining and a very close look at work assignments and budgets, the targets were changed for leverage and productivity, and the staff mix was changed to have two paralegals for each of the attorneys. For 2017, the productivity and leverage numbers will both be collected monthly; calculated quarterly; and reported for partner attorney, nonpartner attorney, and paralegal.

Overall productivity targets were reviewed, and for 2017 the partner target will drop to 75% as each partner needs to take a more active role in client development. When the partners looked at their individual performance KPIs, it was noted that Patty's suspicion was correct. The two partners were recording billed time in excess of 90% when she was close to 70% some months. Since each partner has a different practice, Patty will be helping Philip and Penelope develop new business. This will improve the leverage also as the paralegals are below their target. The paralegals' target should be closer to 90% productivity, and the attorneys will have their overall total hours reduced, but their target is 90% productivity.

With a full year of leverage information for the now four paralegals and attorneys, the partners are rebudgeting their new cases to target higher percentage of involvement by attorneys and paralegals. All small cases are headed up by an attorney, as opposed to a partner, but adequately supervised. With data, the hiring decisions are easier. With a pipeline focused on larger cases, the partners are considering hiring a third attorney but will wait for the first quarter results in 2017. Also, Philip is investigating the use of some affordable e-discovery platforms that will improve everyone's efficiency. Leveraging technology will allow PRODUCT LIT to remain competitive and take on more work.

PRODUCT LIT 2016	PARTNER	ATTORNEYS	PARALEGALS
Productivity (%)	**82%**	**87%**	**77%**
TARGET -Productivity (%)	80%	80%	80%
Input total #billed hours	5401	3474	4100
Input total #timekeepers	3	2	4
Input total hours available	2200	2000	1600

Exhibit 1—Productivity PRODUCT LIT 2016

PRODUCTIVITY													
PROD LIT 2016	Jan	Feb	Mar	Apr	May	June	July	Aug	Sept	Oct	Nov	Dec
3-PROD(a) Client Pipeline (#)	14	13	14	15	12	10	6	4	7	9	9	8
TARGET - Client Pipeline (#)	10	10	10	10	10	10	10	10	10	10	10	10
Input - total number of active firm clients	72	66	70	73	61	50	32	20	35	44	45	42
Input - total attorneys	5	5	5	5	5	5	5	5	5	5	5	5

PROD LIT 2016	Jan	Feb	Mar	Apr	May	June	July	Aug	Sept	Oct	Nov	Dec
3-PROD(b) Revenue per Matter ($)	$ 2,267	$ 2,794	$ 1,929	$ 2,027	$ 3,115	$ 4,545	$ 8,824	$ 4,853	$ 6,000	$ 7,500	$ 3,723	$ 5,682
TARGET - Revenue per Matter ($)	$ 5,000	$ 5,000	$ 5,000	$ 2,500	$ 2,500	$ 2,500	$ 4,000	$ 4,000	$ 4,000	$ 5,000	$ 5,000	$ 5,000
Input - Total Revenue for all matters	$ 170,000	$ 190,000	$ 135,000	$ 150,000	$ 190,000	$ 250,000	$ 300,000	$ 165,000	$ 210,000	$ 345,000	$ 175,000	$ 250,000
Input - # Open matters	75	68	70	74	61	55	34	34	35	46	47	44

PRODUCT LIT 2016	Jan	Feb	Mar	Apr	May	June	July	Aug	Sept	Oct	Nov	Dec
3-PROD(c) Rent Expense (%)	3.1%	2.7%	4.8%	4.7%	3.6%	2.9%	2.4%	3.8%	3.4%	2.1%	4.1%	2.9%
TARGET - Rent Expense (%)	3.0%	3.0%	3.0%	3.0%	3.0%	3.0%	3.0%	3.0%	3.0%	3.0%	3.0%	3.0%
Input - Rent expense	$ 5,500	$ 5,500	$ 7,500	$ 7,500	$ 7,500	$ 7,500	$ 7,500	$ 7,500	$ 7,500	$ 7,500	$ 7,500	$ 7,500
Total Revenue per Financial Statements	$ 180,000	$ 205,000	$ 155,000	$ 160,000	$ 210,000	$ 260,000	$ 310,000	$ 195,000	$ 220,000	$ 355,000	$ 185,000	$ 260,000

PRODUCT LIT 2016	Jan	Feb	Mar	Apr	May	June	July	Aug	Sept	Oct	Nov	Dec
3-PROD(d) Attorney Leverage (%)		92%				86%			81%			81%
TARGET - Attorney Leverage (%)		90%				85%			70%			70%
Input total billings by all attorneys*	$ 150,000	$ 175,000	$ 130,000	$ 130,000	$ 165,000	$ 210,000	$ 260,000	$ 120,000	$ 165,000	$ 285,000	$ 140,000	$ 200,000
Input total billings by firm	$ 170,000	$ 190,000	$ 135,000	$ 150,000	$ 190,000	$ 250,000	$ 300,000	$ 165,000	$ 210,000	$ 345,000	$ 175,000	$ 250,000

Deep Dive KPI 3: Productivity (PROD) § 6:7

PRODUCT LIT 2016	Jan	Feb	Mar	Apr	May	June	July	Aug	Sept	Oct	Nov	Dec
3-PROD(e) Paralegal Leverage (%)			8%			14%			19%			19%
TARGET - Paralegal Leverage (%)			10%			15%			30%			30%
Input total billings by all paralegals*	$ 20,000	$ 15,000	$ 5,000	$ 20,000	$ 25,000	$ 40,000	$ 40,000	$ 45,000	$ 45,000	$ 60,000	$ 35,000	$ 50,000

(* can be linked to "PERFORMANCE KPI" tab)

PRODUCT LIT 2016	Jan	Feb	Mar	Apr	May	June	July	Aug	Sept	Oct	Nov	Dec
3-PROD(f) Attorney Productivity (%)	78%	91%	68%									85%
TARGET - Attorney Productivity (%)	80%	80%	80%									80%
Input total #billed attorney hours	625	729	542									8875
Input total #attorneys	5	5	5									5
Input total hours available	160	160	160									2100

PRODUCT LIT 2016	Jan	Feb	Mar	Apr	May	June	July	Aug	Sept	Oct	Nov	Dec
3-PROD(g) Paralegal Productivity (%)	83%	63%	14%									77%
TARGET - Paralegal Productivity (%)	80%	80%	80%									80%
Input total #billed paralegal hours	200	150	50									4100
Input total #paralegals	2	2	3									4
Input total hours available	120	120	120									1600

§ 6:8 Firm example: PRODUCT LIT—Prior year data points

Given that PRODUCT LIT had hired two new paralegals and were shifting their delivery model to improve leverage, gathering 2015 data first was not a priority.

As mentioned above, once 2016 was completed, the partners directed the bookkeeper to compile prior year data for rent expense to compare results. Also, once the partners reviewed the 2016 Revenue per Matter results, the same information was collected for 2015 in the three newly identified categories based on size of the matter.

Pricing

Given the pressure to provide predictability for clients entering litigation, the partners want to pursue the approach piloted by Patty where the client is given an upper limit for the case. The bookkeeper is preparing the revenue for all the 2016 matters and in addition a breakdown of the actual tasks to create a better budget for each size and type of case. The 2015 data will be helpful, but not as useful as 2016 because in the prior year, the firm was only using attorneys to assist the partners, not paralegals. That said, the hours and resulting revenue can be helpful to compare similar cases. For example, will it take significantly fewer hours with a partner or partner and attorney only? And will that hours savings be offset by the higher billing rates? Achieving the right leverage is an art, like pricing, but the KPI data can assist with both pricing and leverage.

§ 6:9 Technology to assist with productivity KPIs

Properly implemented, technology can not only assist with data collection and reduce duplication of tasks, but also improve and streamline law firm workflow or process. Some of the technologythat can be used to assist with productivity KPIs include:

- Excel—to avoid problems with various versions of the same spreadsheet, use a safe shared drive or server and create links between different workbooks and sheets to simplify data input.
- Accounting Software—As accounting for legal services is more complex than the average small business, an accounting system that handles retainers, trust accounting, and modified accrual method may be necessary. Revenue and rent expense are found on the financial statements.

- Legal Practice Management (LPM)—the number of active clients and matters should be generated from the LPM. Time and billing capabilities may be included in the LPM. A firm-wide dashboard with productivity KPIs should be possible, but at this point in time, most small firm LPMs do not include comprehensive KPI dashboards.
- Time and Billing Software—Again, due to the billing complexities and modified accounting methods, time and billing software that is separate from the accounting or LPM system may be necessary. However, the LPM, accounting system, and time and billing must integrate to provide consistent data. The billed hours and the number of billings number can come from the any of the three systems, but data should only have to be entered once by timekeepers.
- Project Management software—Legal or generic program that allows for collaboration and tracking of budgeted versus actual time on tasks so that the project (or case) can be planned, organized, and managed.
- E-discovery software—Electronic discovery software tools are used in litigation to find, preserve, and protect electronic evidence for presentation. There are a range of companies, some cloud-based, that are providing a software platform that assists with the overwhelming amount of information to be reviewed.

A nonexhaustive list of technology resources is in APPENDIX D.

§ 6:10 Common mistakes or pitfalls

The above firm example and other experiences give rise to lessons learned that are set out below as common mistakes or pitfalls to avoid:

- Cash vs. Modified Accrual. Revenue numbers depend on the accounting methodology and can be difficult to figure out if you are on the cash basis. Our goal is to match revenue with costs or efforts. However, although the best information would have perfect matching, sometimes it is better to get started and evaluate the quality of the data after a few months.
- Mixing up billings versus billable hours. Recording the hours on the time sheet is capturing billable hours, but unless you can bill and be fairly certain of collection, these hours are not billings. Productivity is not about billable hours, but rather creating billings that are ultimately collected.
- Thinking that recording hours no longer matters for pricing if you have alternative fee model, such as fixed fees. Captur-

§ 6:10

ing all the hours, even ones that cannot be billed, is critical for running a firm. Rewards and compensation should be structured in such a way that attorneys and paralegals will record all the hours spent on a case. The decision to bill that unbilled time or WIP should be based on the budget or agreement with the client, but invaluable pricing data comes from the actual time spent.

- Difficulty with budgeting milestones. Some litigation, deals, or projects may be difficult to break into discrete tasks that do not overlap. Or it can be difficult to estimate which task or tasks are being completed. Remember to try to simplify as much as possible and create your billing codes to match your milestone tasks. Timekeepers will only have to enter data into one system.
- Too much too soon. If you do have timing differences because of the cash accounting methodology and billing practices, do not spend too much time adjusting the figures. Run some numbers for the prior year and current year to see if it makes a difference to shift the revenue back a month or two to match with the effort or if it is giving you good enough information. After all, you have to practice law first and foremost.

In the next chapter, we continue to look at the firm-wide metrics. We will look at the fourth KPI—Profitability—using a two-lawyer personal injury firm to illustrate measuring firm profitability.

Chapter 7

Deep Dive KPI 4: Profitability (PROF)

§ 7:1 Introduction
§ 7:2 KPI 4—Profitability (PROF) summary
§ 7:3 Data and sources
§ 7:4 —Definitions
§ 7:5 —Calculations
§ 7:6 Background
§ 7:7 Firm example: PROF PI
§ 7:8 —First quarter results
§ 7:9 —Full year results
§ 7:10 —Prior year data points
§ 7:11 Technology to assist with profitability KPIs
§ 7:12 Common mistakes or pitfalls

§ 7:1 Introduction

When speaking of metrics in general, profitability measurements are at the top of the list, but it is usually the traditional profits per partner or utilization statistics. While those profitability measures may be helpful in larger firms, additional KPIs that look at various components of contribution, including how long it takes to bill and collect, are needed in smaller firms.

Realization or conversion to cash is critical to all businesses, regardless of size. Factoring in cash collection timing is important for small firms, actually all firms, but let us first consider the measures that can improve profitability or the bottom line for small law. Our goal with the overall KPI framework is that interested lawyers can learn the business metrics for law or they can pass this framework to the bookkeeper or a staff member who measures firm results.

It bears repeating the note in Chapter 6 on the impact of alternative fee arrangements and recording hours: Regardless of fee structure, the metrics are the same for profitability and productivity—there is a laser focus on cash collection. Alternative fee arrangements are important for survival in a very competitive market but will not alter your KPI implementation. It is important, though, to collect information on nonbillable time. Some firms have moved away from recording these nonbillable

§ 7:1   LAW FIRM KEY PERFORMANCE INDICATORS

hours. The suggestion is not for an onerous nonbillable system, but in order to evaluate the time spend acquiring clients, business or client development time needs to be captured. Remember that nonbillable hours are a lost opportunity for generating revenue, so understanding where all the hours go is critically important.

§ 7:2 KPI 4—Profitability (PROF) summary

The fourth KPI area on Profitability (PROF) contains 11 metrics as outlined in the table below, and APPENDIX B, Comprehensive KPI Listing—KPI 4: Profitability, presents the information in table format with formulas.

4-PROF Metrics	Calculation	Frequency*
4-PROF (a): Return on Owner Equity (Investment) (ROI) (%)	Owner's compensation divided by the gross revenue	Annually
4-PROF (b): Contribution Margin ($)	Gross revenue less direct costs equals contribution margin, measured by either firm, department, or matter level	Monthly
4-PROF (c): Profitability Margin (%)	Total net income divided by total revenue	Monthly
4-PROF (d): Payroll Ratio (%)	Total payroll costs divided by total revenue	Monthly
4-PROF (e): Overhead Ratio (%)	Total expense less payroll costs divided by total revenue	Monthly
4-PROF (f): Aging Tolerance (%)	Total collections within 60 days divided by total billings	Monthly
4-PROF (g): Work in Progress (WIP) Lockup Days (#)	Total days in the period divided by the WIP turnover days, which is the unbilled time (WIP) for the period divided by the average outstanding WIP balance at the beginning and end of the period	Monthly

4-PROF Metrics	Calculation	Frequency*
4-PROF (h): Accounts Receivable (A/R) Lockup Days (#)	Total days in the period divided by the A/R turnover days, which is the billings for the period divided by the average outstanding A/R balance at the beginning and end of the period	Monthly
4-PROF (i): Year over Year Revenue Growth (%)	Current year total gross revenue divided by prior year total gross revenue	Quarterly
4-PROF (j): Revenue per Employee ($)	Collected revenue divided by total number of employees	Annually
4-PROF (k): Revenue per Attorney ($)	Collected revenue divided by the total number of attorneys	Annually

*We recommend that KPIs should be tracked regularly, either monthly, quarterly, or annually, once fully implemented. In the early stages of adoption, the firm should try to collect as much data as possible monthly and do an assessment at the end of the first quarter, including a comparison to the prior year. Some metrics will lend themselves to monthly measurement, while others will be naturally quarterly or annually. However, each firm's situation will be different, and there is simply no right or wrong approach to measurement; therefore, the frequencies listed in the table are only recommendations or examples.

§ 7:3 Data and sources

The majority of this data comes from the accounting system; however, the measurements around unbilled time (WIP) or accounts receivable (A/R), including aging tolerance, may require data from the billing system, whether that is part of the legal practice management (LPM) or a separate time and billing system. Account receivable collection periods must be tracked, and a LPM or accounting system should have the ability to generate aged A/R and unbilled time (WIP) reports. An aging accounts receivable will group the amounts owing or unbilled into months that are tracked in 30-day increments which represent time that your cash is "locked up" and not available to pay your bills.

§ 7:4 Data and sources—Definitions

Revenue can come from several different sources and should be defined to ensure that these measurements are calculated using consistent data. The following terms are defined below to ensure

§ 7:4

that the measurements are done with proper comparisons. Similar to the other KPIs, the definitions can be adapted to the firm's practice and should be reviewed with the bookkeeper, but the goal is consistency.

Gross Revenue—all the revenue that is recognized in the practice. This figure will include revenue from the matter, disbursements, filing fees, court fees, and in some cases technology charges, like research and other third-party products. Also, the gross revenue number includes cocounsel, expert witnesses, special or private investigators, and other outside professional fees. Revenue may also include late fees or interest earned on cash in the bank. Gross revenue includes all the inflows for the firm.

Revenue—this number is the revenue from the matter that includes the effort from within the firm that is recognized by any one of the three accounting methods, accrual, cash, or modified accrual. The amount can be calculated based on hours or flat fees or a contingency basis. In some cases, this revenue may include outside professionals' fees that are passed through to the client. It is important to understand what is included in order to consistently calculate KPIs.

Billings—the amount billed to the client for the matter in that period. The billed amount may or may not generate revenue on the financial statements, depending on the accounting method. See below for more information.

Billable Hours—the hours recorded as billable do not necessarily become billings. The hours may give rise to flat fees being charged or may become billings as hours, but billable hours are not billings and are also independent of revenue.

Contingent Fees—rather than billing by hours or flat fees, the attorney receives a percentage of the settlement or award. Therefore, the billing occurs only when the client receives money.

Retainers—these are not revenue when the cash is received but more of a down payment and held for billings that will occur later.

§ 7:5 Data and sources—Calculations

The three revenue recognition methods listed below and discussed in more detail in Chapter 6 are fundamental to the profitability calculations.

1. Accrual Method—recognizes revenue when the time is recorded.
2. Modified Accrual Method—recognizes revenue when the WIP is billed to clients.

§ 7:5

3. Cash Method—recognizes revenue when the cash is received.

For practitioners that do not have a LPM that calculates the monthly value of unbilled time or work in progress (WIP) and beginning and ending WIP, you can do your calculations using hours and billing rates or an average revenue per hour of effort. Below is an example of how to calculate 4-PROF(g) WIP Lockup Days using the firm average billing rate. This calculation can be done at the firm level or the partner level, like most of the KPIs presented above.

You need the opening balance for WIP based on the hours in WIP at the end of the prior year or according to your financial statements, if you use accrual or modified accrual. Each month the unbilled hours are added to WIP based on the average billing rate, and anything billed from WIP is subtracted at the billing value.

Using January as an example, the opening balance of WIP is $50,000 on the financial statements as of December of the prior year. That $50,000 becomes your opening balance. At the end of January, you have added $82,500 in new WIP, for a total of $133,500 before billings. Only $5,000 is billed, and, therefore, the ending balance in WIP is $127,500.

Once the firm has the WIP in dollars at the end of each month, you can use this formula for 4-PROF(g) WIP Lockup Days: Total days in the year divided by the WIP turnover days, which is the unbilled time, or WIP, for the period divided by the average outstanding WIP balance at the beginning and end of the period.

WIP LOCKUP DAY—HOURS-BASED CALCULATION			
	Jan	Feb	Mar
Input—Total unbilled hours in WIP	300	380	460
Input—Firm average billing rate	275	275	275
WIP in dollars	$82,500	$104,500	$126,500
Input—Total billings	$5,000	$65,000	$75,000
Opening WIP	$50,000	$127,500	$167,000
Closing WIP	$127,500	$167,000	$218,500
WIP LOCKUP DAY—HOURS-BASED CALCUATION	33	41	47

Although this is just a fictitious example, the takeaway would be that the WIP is building and has gone from taking about one month to be billed to over six weeks. Unless there are ongoing cases or projects that cannot be billed yet according to the fee arrangement, the WIP needs to be reviewed and either billed or written off.

§ 7:6 Background

Profitability goals are a personal choice. Not everyone who practices law shares the same goals for their practice and the elusive work-life balance. Attorneys do not all want to make the most money possible. However, measurements around profitability are much more than profits per partner or utilization because more metrics are needed to see what drives the bottom line and the cash in the bank. Without the cash in the firm bank account, you cannot pay the bills. As mentioned before, starting a small firm is like any other business: proper billing and collection procedures are required.

Attorneys make choices in how they would like to run their practices, but at the end of the day, each client matter is a mini income statement. The lifetime collected revenue for each client, less both the cost of client acquisition and the cost of delivery is the contribution to the firm's overhead and profit. Moreover, finally, cash is king because profits on paper are worthless. Just because you send out a bill for $10,000 with costs of $8,000 does not mean that your profit is $2,000. Until that cash is collected, the profit is not assured. This does not mean you should adopt the cash method of accounting, rather you should use retainers and payments up-front as much as possible to reduce your risk of not being paid.

There are 11 profitability KPIs, and depending on the size of your practice, your current level of profitability, and your ultimate plan or vision, you can implement those all at once or in stages. Also, as the firm example below demonstrates, you can tailor the measures to individual partner situations also.

According to information given in several recent presentations at events sponsored by Group Legal Services Association and Evolve Law, average small law firms collect cash anywhere from almost 90 to 150 days after recording the hours. That means that you pay yourself or others to do work in month one and may only collect the cash in month three or later. Poor cash collection can mean that your firm cannot make payroll.

Before we explore our firm example, let us dispel the fallacy that alternative fees such as flat fees or subscriptions will somehow kill the need for tracking billable hours. It is not really "beyond the billable hour" because you still have to record hours on matters to track costs and profitability. Additionally, in some states you need to record hours for ethical purposes, but that is beyond the scope of this book. Flat fees give you the opportunity to increase gross margins as your practice becomes more efficient.

Also, you will still need to record all types of hours, including nonbillable hours, regardless of whether hourly fees are charged or not, because the only way to measure case profitability is to understand the costs, including how much you spent acquiring a new client. Unfortunately, flat or fixed fees do not mean the death of the timesheet for any professional service.

Finally, it is important to understand that all billable hours are created equal. Although you really only want to bill hours that can be collected or realized, that does not mean to leave hours off your timesheet. If you do not record all your efforts, your firm cannot measure the effort needed to deliver. That will impact pricing, whether it is hourly rates or flat fees.

§ 7:7 Firm example: PROF PI

Two personal injury lawyers run a small firm with a part-time legal assistant. Peter Rowan and Owen Freeman were solo attorneys competing against each other for over 20 years. About five years ago, Owen had a health scare, and Peter helped out with his caseload, and as a result they decided to work separately out of the same office. After two years, they combined their practice to become PROF PI and hired Kay, part-time legal assistant, who works about 25 hours per week over five workdays.

Peter specializes in worker's compensation claims but handles all personal injury matters. Owen has deep expertise in wrongful death and accidents involving all means of transportation: motorcycle, cars, boats, etc. Peter is newly divorced with an ex-wife, three children, and alimony payments requiring that he earn $450,000 per year. Owen is married, and his kids are just starting college, but Owen's wife owns a successful software company. Owen only requires about $250,000 per year. Over the past three years, each has drawn anywhere from $200,000 to $350,000 each. Peter is very concerned that he hit the target of $450,000. The two wish to implement additional KPIs around profits to closely watch the upcoming year's performance.

For the past three years, Owen has been trying to employ as much technology as possible, and both have resisted hiring any attorneys or paralegals. Kay, their legal assistant, is proficient in Excel and also prepares all the prebills for their accountant to run in the cloud-based LPM. Monthly billing takes place on the

§ 7:7   Law Firm Key Performance Indicators

last day of the month. If a case settles or finishes in that month, the billing is included in the monthly billing run.

The firm uses Xero for accounting, which integrates with the LPM. Kay's objective is to have the KPIs in an Excel spreadsheet and link the LPM reports to automatically populate the spreadsheet.

Peter and Owen charge most clients based on a contingency fee basis. Their fee structure is 33% of the settlement if the case does not go to trial and 40% of the award if the case goes to trial. The firm pays the expert expenses out of their share of the revenue.

However, over the last six months of 2016, they took on a few smaller cases where they charged a retainer and then clients paid based on billed hours and direct expenses. At this point, Peter charges $400 per hour and Owen bills $300. They want to review their rates because they are using more technology to become efficient. The rates have been the same for the three years that they have been practicing together.

Using the billing rates as conservative estimates, Peter and Owen have calculated the following:

- $450,000 divided by $400 per hour requires Peter to bill 1,125 hours.
- $250,000 divided by $300 per hours means that Owen bills 834 hours.

The three meet on January 2nd to discuss the data and assumptions for KPIs. To start, Kay explains that the notion that Peter and Owen only need 1,125 and 834 hours in billings is incorrect. The resulting total of $450,000 plus $250,000, or $700,000, is only the revenue, not the actual profit available for draws after paying all the expenses. Also, the majority of their business in the past has been contingency work: Over 90% of the billings were based on contingency in 2015.

Peter and Owen confess that they have not been recording all of their hours on the contingency cases when they are working on the weekends. Kay explains that without all the hour data, the measurement will not be as useful.

Action: Everyone agrees to record all their hours on all matters for 2016.

Targets

Kay sets the overall targets based on 2015 financial statement net income results, adjusted for Peter's requirement for additional draws. The partners decide that the firm should be billing $3 million. When Kay presses to ask if that is with all the outside investigator and witness costs, the partners simply do not know nor understand why it makes a difference. They have both just been interested in the top-line revenue, the monthly draws, and, of course, a positive firm net income.

The three decide that they will record the results monthly and review after the first quarter and that Kay will go through and calculate 2014 and 2015 for 4-PROF(a) Return on Investment (ROI), 4-PROF(b) Contribution Margin, and 4-PROF (c) Profitability Margin.

Peter is very interested in the WIP and A/R and would like to set 30-day targets for each. In other words, Peter wants all WIP billed out each month, unless it is for a contingency fee case, and all billing collected by the following month's end.

Kay points out that the majority of the cases will be contingency fee cases; her rough estimate is over 90%. In the past, only Peter and Owen's hours have gone into WIP, and they have tracked the outside professionals, such as expert witnesses, court reporting, etc., using the accounting system.

Action: For 2016, Kay will include these outsider amounts in WIP in the month that the costs are incurred.

§ 7:8 Firm example: PROF PI—First quarter results

Peter and Owen were shocked by the room for improvement in many areas, particularly client collections. Kay reminded them both that "cash is king" and that the collection process needed some work. Also, based on the initial results around contribution margin, she had taken the liberty of analyzing each of Peter and Owen's results in addition to the firm level and had broken down PROF(i) Year over Year Revenue Growth into contingent and retainer clients.

4-PROF(a) Return on Owner Equity (Investment) (ROI).

It was decided that this figure would not be useful for just three months and that it would be measured at the end of the year. The focus was put on the contribution margin and profitability KPIs.

Peter needs his $450,000, so he draws $37,500 per month. Owen continued to draw at $20,000 per month, to yield roughly $240,000. If there is any extra firm net income after those draws, Owen will take the remaining amount to equal Peter's $450,000, with any remaining net income to be invested.

4-PROF(b) Contribution Margin for the first three months:

PROF PI 2016			
	Jan	Feb	Mar
4-PROF(b)(ii) Contribution Margin (%)	49%	15%	36%
TARGET—Contribution Margin (%)	50%	50%	50%
Input—Gross Revenue	$500,000	$70,000	$215,000
Input—Direct Costs	$255,000	$59,500	$137,500
Total Number of Matters	5	3	5

Kay was surprised by the firm's result in January. Based on Peter's large $1 million judgment from a 2015 case that was awarded in January, she thought that the firm would have a larger contribution margin. She decided to dig down to each partner's results.

However, the firm's accountant explained that the contribution margin for a practice with a large amount of contingency work is best done at the matter level anyway, rather than on the monthly revenue and monthly costs. The issue is matching. When a case lasts more than one month, the revenue from the settlement or the award will be recognized a single month, but the direct costs may be spread over many months. Therefore, the large payout, or revenue, is not matched with the total costs.

PROF PI 2016—PR			
	Jan	Feb	Mar
4-PROF(b) Contribution Margin (%)—PR	46%	6%	-275%
TARGET—Contribution Margin (%—PR)	?	?	?
Input—Gross Revenue	$420,000	$40,000	$10,000
Input—Direct Costs	$225,000	$37,500	$37,500
Input—Number of Matters	3	2	2

Kay was not sure what target to use for each partner's contribution margin. After reviewing both partner's results, she decided that she should use 50% for each. For Peter, Kay looked at the results matter by matter to discover any issues.

Peter's results are all over the place because the big cases are feast or famine in terms of revenue, and there is the matching issue that the costs for prior months were in 2015 for the January 2016 settlement. Additionally, Peter is taking a significantly

Deep Dive KPI 4: Profitability (PROF) § 7:8

larger draw than Owen, which reduces his ability to generate positive margin if he does not have any work that is noncontingency. In other words, if he is just putting his hours and the costs of experts into unbilled time (WIP) and he cannot release the WIP and recognize revenue until he is billing for a contingency fee, that means that Peter will have no revenue in months that cases do not settle or complete. March's negative 275% margin is a direct result of the lack of noncontingency work.

Peter's cases yield larger payouts, but he needs to have some retainer or billable-hour type cases to cover his draw and overhead each month. He needs to diversify his practice to take on some work that is retainer-based and profitable. Kay will monitor the noncontingency work to look at the contribution margin by individual matter to focus Peter's client development efforts.

Also, Peter explains that he has not been billing some of the weekend hours to his contingency cases, as he does not see the point because he is not sending out his bills based on those hours. Kay explains that they will use the statistics from the contingency cases to help create the budgets for the retainer or billable-hour cases.

PROF PI 2016—OF			
	Jan	Feb	Mar
4-PROF(b)(i)Contribution Margin (%)—OF	60%	12%	50%
TARGET—Contribution Margin (%) -OF	?	?	?
Input—Gross Revenue	$75,000	$25,000	$200,000
Input—Direct Costs	$30,000	$22,000	$100,000
Input—Number of Matters	2	1	3

Kay notes that Owen's contribution margin is more consistent. Although he does not have as much revenue, $300,000 versus Peter's $470,000, Owen's costs are much lower, at $152,000 versus Peter's $300,000. Peter reviews the first three months' results and realizes that his contribution margin is also lower because he had $195,500 of cocounsel and expert costs from this $1 million case that hit the direct costs in January. These costs were included in the $400,000 award.

Kay discusses this with the accountant, and he explains that Peter's contribution margin percentage is diluted because the expert costs are included in both revenue and direct costs.

§ 7:8   Law Firm Key Performance Indicators

Matter Revenue	$400,000
Matter Direct Costs	$225,000
Matter Contribution Margin	**$175,000 or 44%**

If you remove the $195,500 from revenue and direct costs, the contribution margin percentage increases:

Matter Revenue	$204,500
Matter Direct Costs	$29,500
Matter Contribution Margin	**$175,000 or 86%**

As there are a small number of matters, Kay will run the mini income statements on each 2016 matter to see the percentage contributed but also the absolute dollar amount. For large contingency cases, Kay needs to go back and check the WIP for prior months for those direct costs and billable hours to avoid the matching issue.

The partners agree that Kay will run these mini income statements for each of their top five cases in 2015. Also, Owen has been lax in recording his billable hours for weekend contingency work and agrees to start recording all his hours. In addition, Owen adjusted his rate, so both partners are billing at $400 starting April 1, 2016.

4-PROF(c) Profitability Margin for the first three months:

PROF PI 2016			
	Jan	Feb	Mar
4-PROF(c)Profitability Margin (%)	44%	-25%	26%
TARGET—Profitability Margin (%)	10%	10%	10%
Input—Net Income	$219,000	-$17,500	$56,500
Input—Revenue	$500,000	$70,000	$215,000

Kay looks at the results and runs the monthly financial statements to try to better understand the negative results in February and the wide swing between January and March.

Deep Dive KPI 4: Profitability (PROF) § 7:8

Monthly Financials	Jan	Feb	Mar
WIP	$227,500	$331,500	$352,500
A/R	$531,250	$348,750	$510,000
Billings	$495,000	$65,000	$210,000
Other Revenue	$5,000	$5,000	$5,000
Gross Revenue	$500,000	$70,000	$215,000
Outside Direct Costs in Gross Revenue	$195,500	$-	$78,000
Total Expenses	$23,000	$25,000	$18,000
Payroll	$62,500	$62,500	$62,500
Net Income	**$219,000**	**-$17,500**	**$56,500**

Kay realizes that she is better off using the KPIs for payroll and overhead in conjunction with the contribution margin to put together a more accurate picture of what is causing the swings in profitability.

4-PROF(d) Payroll Ratio for the first three months:

PROF PI 2016			
	Jan	Feb	Mar
4-PROF(d) Payroll Ratio (%)	13%	89%	29%
TARGET—Payroll Ratio (%)	40%	40%	40%
Input—Monthly Payroll Costs	$62,500	$62,500	$62,500
Total Revenue	$500,000	$70,000	$215,000

Kay realizes that the monthly payroll is linked directly to the accounting system, and, therefore, she includes the owners' or partners' amount in the payroll costs when some of that payroll amount is within the direct costs in the contribution margin. She thinks that it is potentially double counting for the KPIs; however, these KPIs are not an income statement. This payroll ratio shows the trends based on revenue.

Any payroll costs from the attorneys included in the direct costs are correctly allocated because the partners' time is directly related to the delivery of the service, but they are also payroll costs. This payroll has to be meet each month, regardless of activity. For example, if Peter and Owen took the same month off in July, the payroll would continue on even though they are not working. This illustrates how it is important to understand that the KPIs are for measuring trends and setting benchmarks; these metrics are not replacements for your financial statement or financial reporting.

4-PROF(e) Overhead Ratio for the first three months:

PROF PI 2016			
	Jan	Feb	Mar
4-PROF(e) Overhead Ratio (%)	5%	36%	8%
TARGET—Overhead Ratio (%)	10%	10%	10%
Input—Monthly Expenses	$23,000	$25,000	$18,000
Total Revenue	$500,000	$70,000	$215,000

Kay again sees wide swings in the monthly expenses as a percentage of revenue, but the expenses themselves are quite constant. Kay realizes that the target percentage should be much lower, but the partners do not agree; they believe that there will be increased advertising and marketing to attract the new, noncontingency clients and want to try to spend more.

In the meeting on the three-month results, it is decided that Kay will do a breakdown of the fixed monthly expenses so that the monthly fixed costs can be calculated by adding together the payroll costs and the monthly expenses. The partners are now aware that they must cover the payroll of $62,500 plus the monthly expenses that include fixed amounts of $16,000. It becomes very important to collect those bills in a timely fashion to ensure enough cash flow in the months that there is not as much revenue.

4-PROF(f) Aging Tolerance for the first three months:

PROF PI 2016			
	Jan	Feb	Mar
4-PROF(f) Aging Tolerance (%)	21%	75%	24%
TARGET—Aging Tolerance (%)	10%	10%	10%
A/R Greater than 60 days	$104,688	$52,313	$51,000
Input—Total Firm Billings*	$495,000	$70,000	$215,000

*(can be linked to "PRODUCTIVITY KPI" tab)

The partners were very surprised by both the percentages and the absolute dollar amounts. Kay suggested that the partners change the terms of payment from 30 days to payable upon receipt. In addition, Kay will not only contact all the clients with A/R over 60 days, but anyone with a balance outstanding for more than 30 days. They will monitor the results and consider changing the KPI in 2017 to monitor A/R greater than 30 days.

4-PROF(g) Work in Progress (WIP) Lockup Days for the first three months:

PROF PI 2016			
	Jan	Feb	Mar
4-PROF(g) WIP Lockup Days (#)	21	47	45
TARGET—WIP Lockup Days (#)	30	30	30
Input—Total Unbilled Time for the Period*	$407,500	$174,000	$236,000
Input -WIP Balance Beginning of the Period	$320,000	$227,500	$331,500
Input -WIP Balance End of the Period	$227,500	$331,500	$352,500

includes the outside costs and fees

Kay was pleased with the results from the first three months, but Peter was not happy with the February and March results. He wanted everything billed within the first 30 days, and since the matters are billed monthly, he did not understand the lockup day results for February and March. Kay explained that the billings were done on time each month. However, the WIP balance builds up when a case is an ongoing contingency matter until it settles or there is an award. The billing process was reviewed, and Kay recommended that when a case settles that the billing should be done immediately rather than waiting to the end of the month. Both partners agree, and Kay will work with the accountant to issue these bills.

4-PROF(h) Accounts Receivable (A/R) Lockup Days for the first three months:

PROF PI 2016			
	Jan	**Feb**	**Mar**
4-PROF(h) A/R Lockup Days (#)	20	182	62
TARGET—A/R Lockup Days (#)	15	15	15
Input—Total Billings for the Period*	$500,000	$70,000	$215,000
Input—A/R Balance Beginning of the Period	$125,000	$531,250	$348,750
Input—A/R Balance End of the Period	$531,250	$348,750	$510,000

* (can be linked to "PRODUCTIVITY KPI" tab)

Kay consults with their accountant on these surprising results. The A/R balance at the end of 2015 was $125,000, and that has grown to over $500,000 by the end of March. The significant win in January was part of the reason for the increase. That win took place in the second week of January, and with the new, immediate billing, chances are better that it would have been collected.

The accountant explains that the 182 days in February was as a result of the low billing and high A/R balance in comparison. He cautioned that the formula for the calculation will give large variations due to the swings in billings. For a firm like PROF PI, it is better to look at the results over at least a quarter, particularly after big wins.

Owen thought that the settled or complete cases were billed immediately and that collection was within 15 days. Kay explained that the bills were going out with payment terms of net 30 days, but as outlined above, they will switch over to due upon receipt. They also agreed to adjust the target to 30 days for the remainder of 2016.

Kay decides to add WIP and A/R lockup days and makes a new KPI called "Total Lockup Days" to show the number of days from recording the billable hours to receiving the cash.

Deep Dive KPI 4: Profitability (PROF) § 7:8

PROF PI 2016			
	Jan	Feb	Mar
4-PROF (g) Work in Progress & (h) Accounts Receivable TOTAL Lockup Days (#)	41	229	107
TARGET—TOTAL Lockup Days (#)	45	45	45

Kay realizes that this is an average or estimate and that the 4-PROF(f) Aging Tolerance provides the best information on the accounts that are beyond 60 days. She will continue to track this new KPI to show the partners the impact of the billing and collection policy changes.

4-PROF(i) Year over Year Revenue Growth for the first three months:

PROF PI 2016			
	Jan	Feb	Mar
4-PROF(i) Year over Year Revenue Growth CONTINGENCY(%)	198%	55%	168%
TARGET—Year over Year Revenue Growth (%)	110%	110%	110%
Input—Current Year Gross Revenue CONTINGENCY	$495,000	$52,500	$210,000
Input—Prior Year Gross Revenue	$250,000	$95,000	$125,000
4-PROF(i) Year over Year Revenue Growth BILLED HOURS (%)	0%	1250000%	0%
TARGET—Year over Year Revenue Growth (%)	125%	125%	125%
Input—Current Year Gross Revenue RETAINER	$-	$12,500	$-
Input—Prior Year Gross Revenue	$-	$-	$-

When the partners met to set targets, Kay proposed that year over year revenue growth should be isolated for contingency work versus the noncontingency work. The latter is billed based on billable hours and, in some cases, a retainer. Therefore, the revenue can be earned each month, when the work is performed, as opposed to revenue being earned only when the case ends.

4-PROF(j) Revenue per Employee and 4-PROF(k) Revenue per Attorney:

These are annual measures, and given the small size of the firm, it only makes sense to calculate at year's end.

§ 7:9 Firm example: PROF PI—Full year results

Exhibit 1 at the end of the chapter shows all the profitability KPIs for 2016. In past years, Kay would have analyzed results by looking at the 2016 income statement below plus the ending A/R balance of $376,500. Note that the partners' salaries are only in one place on the income statement, included in Payroll.

2016 Billings	$2,405,000
Other Revenue	$79,000
Gross Revenue	**$2,484,000**
Outside Direct Costs in Gross Revenue	$578,000
Total Expenses	$356,000
Payroll	$750,000
	$1,684,000
Net Income	$800,000

This year, a quick review of the figures showed a mixed picture. Overall, the billings were well short of the $3 million target, but there was $800,000 left over after draws that allowed for Owen to also take an additional $210,000 to match Peter's $450,000 draw. The remaining income was set aside in the partnership.

4-PROF(a) Return on Owner Equity (Investment) was 37% for the year based on the two partners each drawing $450,000 as their return on the revenue of $2,405,000. The original goal was 40%, but each partner was happy with their draws, and there was additional income left in the practice. In fact, if all the income was distributed to the partners from the firm as draws for the year after the initial draws of $450,000, the ROI would rise to 62%.

Thus, the partners were a bit confused as to how to measure a successful year: Is it revenue? Cash? Net income? Kay walked the partners through the results, and the range of profitability KPIs allowed Kay to pinpoint success and also areas for improvement in 2017.

Next, the partners reviewed the firm contribution margin and their individual results. Looking at the month-by-month results, the firm rose steadily after the first quarter. There was a low of 12% in April, but several months were over the 50% target. On average for the year, the number was 48%.

Deep Dive KPI 4: Profitability (PROF) § 7:9

However, when Kay presented Peter's and Owen's individual results, the difference was almost 20%. Peter's contribution margin was 37%, and Owen's was 55% for the year with the outside costs included in the revenue and costs for both partners. The variables impacting the results include the settlement or award amount, the revenue from the billings and the amount spent on outsiders, and either Peter's or Owen's time.

Kay pulled out the direct costs because they are pass through revenue and were diluting the contribution margin. Clients pay for the medical reports, expert witnesses and investigators, court reporter, and other deposition costs, although PROF PI pays these fees first.

Kay had already run the yearly numbers with the outsider costs removed, and as could be expected, both partners' results improved, but Owen's numbers improved more, as he had taken less of a draw over the year until the final financial statements were prepared. Kay adjusted for the equal draw, and the partners' contributions were closer, Peter at 43% and Owen at 49%.

However, removing the outsider costs that were reimbursed by clients showed that Peter's costs were higher than Owen's by about $30,000 and that Owen had approximately $47,000 additional revenue. When they discussed these direct costs over and above their equal draws, Owen was averaging about $2,000 per month, and Peter's costs ranged from $3,000 to $5,000. In total, Peter's nonreimbursed outside costs were $55,000 against Owen's $24,000.

Owen used technology to help with document generation, filing, depositions, serving clients, and organizing the exhibits that averaged the $2,000 per month for software licenses. Owen can scale up his practice without any significant impact on this monthly amount, whereas, Peter is paying outside contractors on a project or hourly basis, and the more work, these costs will increase.

The three decided it is also important to look at not just percentages but also absolute dollars for any measure. The bottom line is that Owen contributed $463,000 to pay the firm's overhead versus Peter's $385,000. Peter will be looking into the software that Owen is using to be more efficient in 2017 as they both try to grow the firm.

Kay now has the five largest contingency matters for 2016 to calculate the mini income statements to see the contribution in both absolute dollars and percentage to review at their next meeting.

The partners were happy that the noncontingency work has

grown from 7% of the revenue to 15% of the practice revenue for the year ended 2016. The growth has taken place in the last couple of quarters. Kay cautions the partners that only cases where there will be a positive contribution should be taken. In 2016, the partners had less than 10 retainer cases between them, totally about $357,000 of revenue. Both would like mini income statements run on those cases because it will help with pricing, including billing rates. Kay will ask the accountant to pull the information from the LPM because both partners billed all their time appropriately for all noncontingency matters in 2016.

Also, given the nature of the contingency work, Kay believes that a separate 4-PROF(b) Contribution Margin should be run on all the cases that were lost in 2016 because, at this point, Peter and Owen's time on those cases are included in the direct costs for all their matters.

In other words, Kay would like to split up the contingency matter direct costs results by removing the direct costs that will never be recovered, those for lost cases. Since the client still has to pay the normally reimbursable outsider costs regardless of outcome, Kay is looking to see how much time or money were spent on these cases that had to be written off when the case was lost because, at this point, the time and nonreimbursed costs are included in the overall firm and individual partner costs. With those amounts and the outsider costs removed from the results, Kay will be able to analyze the true direct costs of the contingency cases and, therefore, the proper margin. However, these costs are a part of the overall cost of doing business because it cannot be assumed that every contingency case will result in a settlement or win. The contingency case information on direct costs can then be used to evaluate the billable rates.

Kay also discussed the fee structure with the accountant because she has heard that other attorneys are paying the expenses first before applying their contingency percentage. The accountant showed Kay how that would increase the contribution margin but not the revenue, using Peter's $1 million award case with $195,500 of cocounsel and direct costs as an example.

Current Method for $1M Award

Award	$1,000,000
Matter Revenue (40%)	**$400,000**
Matter Direct Costs	$225,000
Matter Contribution Margin	**$175,000, or 44%**

New Method for $1M Award

If you remove the $195,500 from the award before applying the percentage.

Award	$1,000,000
Outside Costs	$195,500
Available for Fees	$804,500
Matter Revenue (40%)	**$321,800**
Matter Direct Costs	$29,500
Matter Contribution Margin	**$292,300, or 91%**

The partners discuss doing an analysis of the contribution margin for the last three years to see if there are any differences in the types of cases. For example, what are the margins on workers' compensation cases versus insurance or wrongful death. This information can inform any future flat fees and help the partners decide where to focus their advertising campaigns.

The lockup days KPIs, including Kay's new total, show improvement over the year. The WIP lockup is quite constant. The new billing as soon as the case settles or is complete has improved the average. There were still some spikes in the A/R lock days that occurred when the A/R balance was large and the billings low in the following month. Kay knew to then look to 4-PROF(f) Aging Tolerance, which had the A/R over 60 days trending below 10%, with the exception of October. Kay had made calls to collect the A/R over 60 days after October's result.

Overall the partners decide that although they did not hit their revenue target of $3 million, that was not important because their individual goals as far as draws were actually exceeded.

Proposed Changes

Contingency Fee Structure—Kay proposed a change to the fee structure so that the firm would receive 33% of the settlement or 40% of the award after the expenses are paid. Therefore, the expenses would come off the award before the firm percentage is applied. The partners want to do some research in their area to see if other attorneys in the market follow this practice and, more importantly, whether their clients will accept this change.

Retainer Cases—Both attorneys are billing at $400 per hour. Kay is going to run more data from 2015 on the hours spent on the cases to try to group the types of cases and determine some budgets that could eventually lead to flat fees for more routine matters.

Billing & Collection Process—Kay will run a prebill immediately when a case settles and will no longer wait until month's end. She will also discuss e-billing, automated follow-up, and collections with the accountant, as the firm LPM may integrate with some solutions that can bring the cash into the bank account more quickly using technology.

Direct Costs Allocation—Direct costs will be allocated to the matters at the partner's draw rate based on the time sheets. 4—PROF(d) Payroll Ratio still includes the partners' draw, as they are part of payroll. If the partners were not spending any of their time on matters, then they would not have any time in direct costs. It would all be only in payroll. Firms should not mix up the financial statement accounting with the KPIs.

Annual Billing Rate Review—based on the current year's data, Kay will propose new rates in 2017, but both partners will continue to have the same rates as each other. More detail is included below under the pricing section.

Training for Kay—the accountant suggested that once Kay is trained on the KPIs, she should run the reports and prepare the KPI reports for the partners each month because it is more effective. Also, Kay understands the practice workflows and day to day better than the accountant and is genuinely interested in improving the practice.

Pricing

It is important to not forget that, regardless of cost buildup to a billable hour rate or a flat fee your fees are ultimately determined by what the market can bear. If your rates or flat fees are too expensive, clients will not pay and you may need to review your costs while reducing your rates.

The profitability KPIs are helpful for pricing because you can glean some averages from your costs as ratios to see what your billable rate should be to achieve your target net income. Let's use Peter's data from above as an example. We can build up what the rate should be or break down Peter's current rate, or a combination. Both approaches have used the income statement approach, where revenue is 100%, and then the contribution margin. Peter's hourly billable rate is $400, and his draws, or salary, total $450,000.

Build Up Current Hourly Rate:

Using the standard workdays and hours approach, Peter's

Deep Dive KPI 4: Profitability (PROF) § 7:9

$450,000 salary is divided by 2,080 hours, which translates into $216 per hour. Direct costs are approximately 49% of revenue, and the payroll after removing Peter and Owen is 1% of revenue. Remember that because Peter's draw, or payroll cost, is included in the direct cost line, the payroll should only be Kay. Peter is not covering Owen's payroll. Finally, the overhead is 15% of revenue to realize a 35% net income.

Direct Costs	$212
Payroll & Overhead	$ 69
	$281 Before Net Income
Net Income	$151
Calculated Billing Rate	$432

The $432 is what is required to cover the costs with a 35% net income. However, the current rate is $400, so assuming that the costs are the same as above, the net income would be $119 instead of $151. Again, if the market will only bear $400, your rate is $400. Pricing is an art informed by math and governed by your clients.

We will also address pricing under the next KPI performance.

Exhibit 1—Profitability PROF PI 2016

PROFITABILITY	Jan	Feb	Mar	Apr	May	June	July	Aug	Sept	Oct	Nov	Dec
PROF PI 2016												
4-PROF(a) Return on Owner Equity (investment) (%)	46%	6%	-275%	-7%	50%	37%	39%	50%	32%	40%	44%	37%
TARGET - Return on Owner Equity (investment) (%)		?	?	50%	50%	50%	50%	50%	50%	50%	50%	40%
Input: owner or partner compensation												$ 900,000
Input: annual gross revenue												$2,405,000
PROF PI 2016 - PR												
4-PROF(b) Contribution Margin (%) - PR	46%	6%	-275%	-7%	50%	37%	39%	50%	32%	40%	44%	35%
TARGET - Contribution Margin (% - PR)	50%	?	?	50%	50%	50%	50%	50%	50%	50%	50%	50%
Input - Gross Revenue	$ 420,000	$ 40,000	$ 10,000	$ 35,000	$ 75,000	$ 75,000	$ 90,000	$ 75,000	$ 95,000	$ 75,000	$ 90,000	$ 100,000
Input - Direct Costs	$ 225,000	$ 37,500	$ 37,500	$ 32,500	$ 37,500	$ 47,500	$ 55,000	$ 37,500	$ 50,000	$ 45,000	$ 50,000	$ 65,000
Input - Number of Matters	3	2	2	2	3	3	2	2	2	2	3	2
PROF PI 2016 - OF												
4-PROF(b)(i) Contribution Margin (%) - OF	60%	12%	50%	12%	31%	51%	31%	58%	65%	55%	58%	12%
TARGET - Contribution Margin (%)			50%	50%	50%	50%	50%	50%	50%	50%	50%	50%
Input - Gross Revenue	$ 75,000	$ 25,000	$ 200,000	$ 25,000	$ 32,000	$ 45,000	$ 32,000	$ 80,000	$ 500,000	$ 101,000	$ 85,000	$ 25,000
Input - Direct Costs	$ 30,000	$ 22,000	$ 100,000	$ 22,000	$ 22,000	$ 22,000	$ 22,000	$ 34,000	$ 175,000	$ 45,000	$ 36,000	$ 22,000
Input - Number of Matters	2	1	3	5	5	5	4	3	2	1	3	5
PROF PI 2016												
4-PROF(b)(i) Contribution Margin (%)	49%	15%	36%	12%	47%	44%	43%	55%	60%	51%	53%	35%
TARGET - Contribution Margin (%)	50%	50%	50%	50%	50%	50%	50%	50%	50%	50%	50%	50%
Input - Gross Revenue	$ 500,000	$ 70,000	$ 215,000	$ 67,500	$ 112,000	$ 125,000	$ 135,500	$ 160,000	$ 600,000	$ 183,000	$ 183,000	$ 133,000
Input - Direct Costs	$ 255,000	$ 59,500	$ 137,500	$ 59,500	$ 59,500	$ 69,500	$ 77,000	$ 71,500	$ 240,000	$ 90,000	$ 86,000	$ 87,000
Total Number of Matters	5	3	5	7	8	8	6	5	4	3	6	7
PROF PI 2016												
4-PROF(c) Profitability Margin (%)	44%	-25%	26%	-27%	16%	16%	17%	38%	55%	11%	39%	14%
TARGET - Profitability Margin (%)	10%	10%	10%	10%	10%	10%	10%	10%	10%	10%	10%	10%
Input - Net income	219,000	$ 17,500	$ 56,500	$ 18,000	$ 17,500	$ 20,500	$ 22,500	$ 60,500	$ 330,000	$ 20,000	$ 71,000	$ 18,000
Input - Revenue	$ 500,000	$ 70,000	$ 215,000	$ 67,500	$ 112,000	$ 125,000	$ 135,500	$ 160,000	$ 600,000	$ 183,000	$ 183,000	$ 133,000
PROF PI 2016												
4-PROF(d) Payroll Ratio (%)	13%	89%	29%	93%	56%	50%	46%	39%	10%	34%	34%	47%
TARGET - Payroll Ratio (%)	40%	40%	40%	40%	40%	40%	40%	40%	40%	40%	40%	40%
Input monthly payroll costs total	$ 62,500	$ 62,500	$ 62,500	$ 62,500	$ 62,500	$ 62,500	$ 62,500	$ 62,500	$ 62,500	$ 62,500	$ 62,500	$ 62,500
Total Revenue	$ 500,000	$ 70,000	$ 215,000	$ 67,500	$ 112,000	$ 125,000	$ 135,500	$ 160,000	$ 600,000	$ 183,000	$ 183,000	$ 133,000
PROF PI 2016												
4-PROF(e) Overhead Ratio (%)	5%	36%	8%	34%	29%	26%	24%	16%	5%	38%	13%	19%
TARGET - Overhead Ratio (%)	10%	10%	10%	10%	10%	10%	10%	10%	10%	10%	10%	10%
Input Monthly Expenses	$ 23,000	$ 25,000	$ 18,000	$ 23,000	$ 32,000	$ 32,000	$ 33,000	$ 25,000	$ 27,000	$ 70,000	$ 23,000	$ 25,000
Total Revenue	$ 500,000	$ 70,000	$ 215,000	$ 67,500	$ 112,000	$ 125,000	$ 135,500	$ 160,000	$ 600,000	$ 183,000	$ 183,000	$ 133,000
PROF PI 2016												
4-PROF(f) Aging Tolerance (%)	21%	75%	24%	7%	31%	47%	22%	4%	9%	100%	11%	14%
TARGET - Aging Tolerance (%)	10%	10%	10%	10%	10%	10%	10%	10%	10%	10%	10%	10%
A/R greater than 60 days	$ 104,688	$ 52,313	$ 51,000	$ 4,860	$ 34,500	$ 58,800	$ 29,500	$ 6,535	$ 54,675	$ 183,500	$ 20,450	$ 18,825
Input - total firm billings*	$ 495,000	$ 70,000	$ 215,000	$ 67,500	$ 112,000	$ 125,000	$ 135,500	$ 160,000	$ 600,000	$ 183,000	$ 183,000	$ 133,000

Deep Dive KPI 4: Profitability (PROF) § 7:9

PROF PI 2016	Jan	Feb	Mar	Apr	May	June	July	Aug	Sept	Oct	Nov	Dec	Annual
4-PROF(g)WIP Lockup Days (#)	21	47	45	90	85	91	106	107	31	34	48	54	56
TARGET - WIP Lockup Days (#)	30	30	30	30	30	30	30	30	30	30	30	30	30
Input - Total Unbilled Time for the period*	$174,000	$174,000	$236,000	$128,000	$160,000	$158,000	$145,500	$144,000	$360,500	$270,100	$222,500	$247,500	$2,653,600
Input -WIP balance beginning of the period	$320,000	$227,500	$331,500	$352,500	$413,000	$461,000	$494,000	$504,000	$488,000	$248,500	$335,600	$375,100	$320,000
Input -WIP balance end of the period	$227,500	$331,500	$352,500	$413,000	$461,000	$494,000	$504,000	$488,000	$248,500	$335,600	$375,100	$489,600	$489,600

*includes the outside costs and fees

PROF PI 2016	Jan	Feb	Mar	Apr	May	June	July	Aug	Sept	Oct	Nov	Dec	Annual
4-PROF(h)A/R Lockup Days (#)	20	182	62	221	147	140	135	120	44	155	94	92	37
TARGET - A/R Lockup Days (#)	15	15	15	30	30	30	30	30	30	30	30	30	15
Input - Total billings for the period*	$500,000	$70,000	$215,000	$67,500	$112,500	$125,000	$135,500	$160,000	$600,000	$183,000	$183,000	$133,000	$2,484,000
Input -A/R balance beginning of the period	$125,000	$531,250	$348,750	$510,000	$486,000	$575,000	$588,000	$590,000	$653,500	$1,093,500	$734,000	$409,000	$125,000
Input -A/R balance end of the period	$531,250	$348,750	$510,000	$486,000	$575,000	$588,000	$590,000	$653,500	$1,093,500	$734,000	$409,000	$376,500	$376,500

(* can be linked to "PRODUCTIVITY KPI" tab)

PROF PI 2016	Jan	Feb	Mar	Apr	May	June	July	Aug	Sept	Oct	Nov	Dec
4-PROF(i)Year over Year Revenue Growth CONTINGENCY	198%	55%	168%			42%			102%			75%
TARGET - Year over Year Revenue Growth (%)	110%	110%	110%			110%			110%			110%
Input - current year gross revenue	$495,000	$52,500	$210,000	$25,000	$82,000	$88,000	$97,000	$80,000	$470,000	$171,000	$162,500	$115,000
Input - prior year gross revenue	$250,000	$95,000	$125,000	$400,000	$25,000	$40,000	$35,000	$250,000	$350,000	$200,000	$350,000	$50,000
4-PROF(j)Year over Year Revenue Growth BILLED HOURS	0%	1250000%	0%			245%			366%			46%
TARGET - Year over Year Revenue Growth (%)	125%	125%	125%			125%			125%			125%
Input - current year gross revenue RETAINER		$12,500		$35,000	$25,000	$32,000	$25,000	$75,000	$125,000	$5,000	$12,500	$10,000
Input - prior year gross revenue				$25,000		$12,500	$1,500	$45,000	$15,000	$5,000	$50,000	$5,000

PROF PI 2016	Jan	Feb	Mar	Apr	May	June	July	Aug	Sept	Oct	Nov	Dec
4-PROF(j)Revenue per Employee ($)												$3,848,000
TARGET - Revenue per Employee ($)												$3,000,000
Input average number of annual employees												0.625

PROF PI 2016	Jan	Feb	Mar	Apr	May	June	July	Aug	Sept	Oct	Nov	Dec
4-PROF(k)Revenue per Attorney ($)												$1,202,500
TARGET - Revenue per Attorney ($)												$1,500,000
Input average number of annual attorneys												2

PROF PI 2016	Jan	Feb	Mar	Apr	May	June	July	Aug	Sept	Oct	Nov	Dec	Annual
4-PROF (g)&(h) TOTAL Lockup Days (#)	41	229	107	311	232	230	241	227	74	188	142	146	93
TARGET - TOTAL Lockup Days (#)	45	45	45	60	60	60	60	60	60	60	60	60	45

§ 7:10 Firm example: PROF PI—Prior year data points

Overall, the profitability KPIs come from information that is readily available, and the partners ask Kay to work an extra 10 hours for two weeks to gather the data from the past three years.

Kay first pulled the income statements from 2014 and 2015 to look at the ROI, contribution margin, and profitability before diving into the individual partners and matters. She reminded the partners that the results might be skewed because the partners were not recording all of their time when working on cases on the weekend.

2014 Billings	$2,987,000
Other Revenue	$21,000
Gross Revenue	**$3,008,000**
Outside Direct Costs in Gross Revenue	$910,000
Total Expenses	$180,000
Payroll	$935,000
	$2,025,000
Net Income	**$983,000**

2015 Billings	$2,329,000
Other Revenue	$46,000
Gross Revenue	**$2,375,000**
Outside Direct Costs in Gross Revenue	$975,000
Total Expenses	$264,000
Payroll	$735,000
	$1,974,000
Net Income	**$401,000**

The ROI, contribution margin, and profit margin were as follows:

	2016	2015	2014
4-PROF(a) ROI	38%	30%	27%
4-PROF(b) Contribution Margin*	46%	28%	44%
4-PROF(c) Profit Margin	33%	17%	33%

*Includes the direct costs in all three years.

The ROI trend is very positive. Regardless of absolute dollar revenue, the partners are realizing a larger percentage for each dollar earned over the past three years. In 2015, the contribution margin and profit margin dipped. The contribution margin is affected, or more accurately, diluted, as outlined above, by the direct costs being in both revenue and costs. That is something that is changing in 2017, and the accountant will go back through and pull out those direct costs amounts so that the past years can be properly compared at the firm level and then at the partner level.

Kay's goal is to gather more information on the past cases by running the mini income statements for 2016 and 2015. Due to the dip in 2015, the five biggest cases for each partner need to be analyzed, with and without the direct costs, to find the cause of the dip in results.

The partners are very interested in Kay's pursuit of the right mix of cases since they stopped operating independently. Both will focus on having a few small cases to cover the overhead when they are working on larger cases that span numerous months. Kay is being trained on the other KPIs, including client development, in order to ensure an adequate pipeline to mitigate the feast or famine revenue. Kay knows that she cannot predict the outcome of the case, but working on the mix of contingency versus noncontingency matters by proactively trying to increase the latter will help the ROI.

Both partners will review not only the profitability results, but also Peter will be working with Owen's help to implement technology to streamline his practice, particularly for the contingency cases.

§ 7:11 Technology to assist with profitability KPIs

Properly implemented technology can not only assist with data collection and reduce duplication of tasks, but also improve and streamline law firm workflow or process. Some of the technology that can be used to assist with profitability KPIs include:

- Excel—to avoid problems with various versions of the same spreadsheet, use a safe shared drive or server, and create links between different workbooks and sheets to simplify data input. If you can regularly export an Excel or csv file from its time and billing system, accounting, or LPM, you can then link that file to your KPI spreadsheet to avoid duplicate data entry.
- Accounting Software—As accounting for legal services is more complex than the average small business, an account-

ing system that handles retainers, trust accounting, and modified accrual method may be necessary.
- Time and Billing Software—Again, due to the billing complexities and modified accounting methods, time and billing software is often necessary. If a firm is using multiple systems, interoperability is important. The LPM, accounting system, and time and billing must integrate to provide consistent data.
- E-discovery software—Electronic discovery software tools are used in litigation to find, preserve, and protect electronic evidence for presentation. There are a range of companies, some cloud-based, that are providing a software platform that assists with the overwhelming amount of information to be reviewed.
- Deposition software—Cloud-based software can help with sharing facts on the case, taking live depositions without travel, and serving subpoenas using a mobile application.

A nonexhaustive list of technology resources is in APPENDIX D.

§ 7:12 Common mistakes or pitfalls

The above firm example and other experiences give rise to lessons learned that are set out below as common mistakes or pitfalls to avoid:
- Not taking the cash up front. Wherever possible and allowable, always take the cash up front in the form of a retainer. Some states allow an evergreen retainer which auto replenishes the retainer each month.
- Ignoring collection technology. Not only are there are e-billing solutions that deliver invoices immediately and electronically, but there are also integrated automated invoice follow-up products. In addition, there are products that help you get an A/R advance. All these speed up the time to receive the cash.
- Having analysis paralysis. Start with the broadest measurements and take a more detailed look if there are problem areas or strange trends. Create a dashboard that has some red flags to monitor measures that are critical to your firm but do not start at the most granular level. In other words, check the overall firm results before diving into a detailed review at the individual department or attorney level. Top down works for this KPI.
- Double counting partner's salaries or draws as both a direct and payroll cost. Partners' salaries are a direct cost when

they are working on a matter, but when you are looking at the income statement, generally that amount is included in payroll. Care must be taken when analyzing KPIs or creating pricing models to not double count the partners' draw or attorney and paralegal salaries.
- Operating at the wrong level. In a small business, a CEO does not usually do the accounting. Delegate tasks around routine billing and client follow-up to a legal or administrative assistant.
- Getting caught up in ratios or percentages. Remember that the absolute dollar amounts are important, and these percentages can show trends and alert you to where more analysis is required.

In the next chapter we shift gears and look at the individual timekeepers' contribution to the firm. We will look at the fifth KPI—Performance in a real estate firm with three attorneys, two paralegals, and a billable administrative assistant.

Chapter 8

Deep Dive KPI 5: Performance (PERF)

§ 8:1 Introduction
§ 8:2 KPI 5—Performance (PERF) summary
§ 8:3 Data and sources
§ 8:4 Background
§ 8:5 Firm example: PERFORM REAL ESTATE
§ 8:6 —First quarter results
§ 8:7 —Full year results
§ 8:8 —Prior year data points
§ 8:9 Technology to assist with performance KPIs
§ 8:10 Common mistakes or pitfalls

§ 8:1 Introduction

The firm's performance is comprised of the individual efforts and alignment of those efforts with targets set for those individuals. Timekeepers must work within the firm culture, and their efforts directly impact the client experience. The goal of the fifth KPI is to ensure that performance measurement and targets are aligned with the firm vision for delivering value to clients. Success will not be measured solely by the number hours recorded or billed. Once you start measuring timekeeper performance, softer issues around client service and delivery as well as firm culture will surface. Therefore, in practice, the remaining three KPIs, performance, client experience, and firm culture should be examined together and not in isolation.

§ 8:2 KPI 5—Performance (PERF) summary

The fifth KPI area on Performance (PERF) contains eight metrics as outlined in the table below, and APPENDIX B, Comprehensive KPI Listing—KPI 5: Performance, presents the information in table format with formulas.

5-PERF Metrics	Calculation	Frequency**
5-PERF (a): Billings Collected by Attorney (%)	Total dollars collected by attorney divided by the total billings by attorney	Monthly
5-PERF (b): Billings Collected by Paralegal* or Admin (%)	Total dollars collected by paralegal divided by the total billings by paralegal	Monthly
5-PERF (c): Net Collection by Attorney ($/Hour)	Total dollars collected by attorney divided by the available hours by attorney	Monthly
5-PERF (d): Net Collection by Paralegal* or Admin ($/Hour)	Total dollars collected by paralegal divided by the available hours by paralegal	Monthly
5-PERF (e): Hourly Billings by Attorney ($/Hour)	Total billings by attorney divided by the actual billed hours by attorney	Monthly
5-PERF (f): Hourly Billings by Paralegal* or Admin ($/Hour)	Total billings by paralegal divided by the actual billed hours by paralegal	Monthly
5-PERF (g): Hourly Revenue Collected by Attorney ($/Hour)	Total dollars collected by attorney divided by the actual billed hours by attorney	Annually
5-PERF (h): Hourly Revenue Collected by Paralegal* or Admin ($/Hour)	Total dollars collected by paralegal divided by the actual billed hours by paralegal	Annually

* Paralegals are not the only nonattorney timekeeper; the KPI can be adjusted for legal assistants, legal secretaries, or administrative assistants that are recording hours on client matters.

** We recommend that KPIs tracked regularly, either monthly, quarterly, or annually, once fully implemented. In the early stages of adoption, try to collect as much data as possible monthly and do an assessment at the end of the first quarter, including a comparison to the prior year. Some metrics will lend themselves to monthly measurement, while others will be naturally quarterly or annually. However, each firm's situation will be different, and there is simply no right or wrong approach to measurement; therefore, the frequencies listed in the table are only recommendations or examples.

§ 8:3 Data and sources

In comparison to the first four KPIs, the data comes from one or, at most, two systems, the timekeeping or accounting system. Of the four inputs for each timekeeper listed below, all come from the time and billing system except perhaps the available hours. Those hours are the time that could be spent on client work, not the total hours in the working year. An example below will help measure comparable inputs to obtain useful performance KPIs plus more information for pricing and budgets.

Dollars Collected by Timekeeper—When the client pays, that should be recorded against the outstanding invoices that relate to the hours billed by the timekeeper. If the client does not pay the entire invoice, then it is easy to figure out that all the timekeepers on the invoice have not been paid for the work. However, if a client disputes part of an invoice, it is important to record what time will be unpaid and, therefore, written off.

Dollars & Actual Hours Billed by Timekeeper—Regardless of accounting methodology, the dollars and hours billed must be captured by the accounting, time and billing, or LPM systems. Some firms that are using the cash method may have the billed hours and the dollars in the LPM, with only the collections in the accounting system.

Available Hours—Often this number is thought of as an annual total and confused with a billable-hour target. To start, you need a firm baseline available hours that can then be adjusted for individual circumstance and finally applied to each month based on the timekeeper's schedule. Below is a simple example of how the baseline is calculated for one firm, and this can be adjusted, depending on the situation. We will carry these numbers through to our firm KPI performance example below.

Available Hours

Starting Point for working hours per year:
40 hours per week for 52 weeks   2,080
Remove:
        Vacation—4 weeks 160 hours
        Holidays—10 days 80 hours
        Sick time—5 days 40 hours   <280>
        1,800

Therefore, each person should be working off of a starting point of 1,800 hours available for client work and other responsibilities.

For example, if as a partner you are responsible for administration and that takes up 10% of your time, then 180 hours should be removed from your available hours. Alternatively, if, as the attorney in charge of new business, you will have a significant amount of client development approaching 50%, then 900 should be removed from your available hours.

The goal is to have a target amount of time that you are available to work on client matters. It is not a billable hour target because, in some cases, the firm may only use contingency or flat fees. For the performance KPI, the objective is to measure billed and collected fees, not just billed, and then, for pricing and budgeting, the PERF KPIs can be used to assist in hourly rates and flat fees.

Timing & Matching Issues

The focus is on the revenue collected or realized. In order to measure the revenue, the accounting methodology again becomes important to understand. In prior chapters, we have laid out when revenue occurs for each of the methods. The goal is to match the cash collected to the amount billed within the measurement period. However, because of the accounting methods and time needed to collect the cash, that match may not be achieved.

The performance KPIs are mostly calculated on a monthly basis. In the case where a firm uses the cash methodology, revenue will not be recognized until the cash is collected. With the accrual method, the revenue occurs when the hours are recorded in WIP. Under modified accrual, the billing triggers the revenue. For the performance KPI, we wish to use the billing amount as the input, regardless of which of the revenue-recognition methods are used.

Accounting policy for revenue recognition aside, the cash collection will most likely not take place within the same month as the billing. However, if the clients pay an upfront retainer, monthly retainer, or a flat monthly, subscription-type fee, there will be perfect matching of the billed amount taken from the retainer or the flat fee paid within the same month.

A flat fee that is paid after the matter is complete will have the same or longer timing gap as monthly billing for the work done in that particular month if the billing is only done at the end and the matter takes more than a month.

Flat fees paid up front have an opposite effect on the relationship between billed and collected. The cash is received before the billing and before any work is done; therefore, there is cash, but nothing to bill nor any revenue. The billing of the flat fee does not mean that you can recognize the revenue; however, it does secure the cash associated with the matter. From the chapter on the productivity KPI, we learned that the revenue is recognized or earned as the work is done and that milestones are reached under the earned value method.

If we are to compare all the timing possibilities, the cash and the amount billed do not match in many cases. Depending on the fluctuations in billing and collections, a decision needs to be made whether the KPI numbers are adjusted for timing or not. To start, gather the data and review it to determine whether any timing difference makes a significant impact; remember our KISS principle. We will explore this further in our firm example below.

§ 8:4 Background

Individual performance is linked to compensation, whether it is employee salaries, contractor rates, or owners' draws. Measuring and tracking performance will drive employee behavior and must be approached as an overall strategy, aligning the targets with the firm vision and focusing on the right measures because otherwise the firm culture will suffer and you run the risk of losing good people.

Traditional utilization performance metrics can focus timekeepers on how many hours are recorded and billed rather than actual realized or collected revenue. Aligning the firm goals with the compensation and performance measurement is critical. Overall delivering excellent client value will be defined firm by firm. However, an overriding principle is that you cannot have your attorneys and paralegals trying to bill as much as possible to meet their performance targets if that does not match your firm's client service philosophy or economics.

For example, clients may wish to have fixed fees or budgets for work and minimize costs. Yet if your attorneys or paralegals are rewarded for hitting billable-hour targets, their goals are to record more hours rather than less. This misalignment will cause problems within the firm and with clients.

Performance KPIs can be coupled with the information from the profitability KPI to look for pricing information from billable-hour rates to flat fees for matters. It is worth repeating that hours need to be recorded even in the case where the firm only bills based on dollars.

The work-product effort is reflected in the hours, and, in some cases, it is the more hours, the better, while in others, the fewer, the better: It is dependent on the firm's business and billing model. It also depends on the use of technology because software can save time. That time savings can sometimes mean fewer billable hours, but perhaps that allows the firm to compete. Alternatively, in other cases, perhaps you can charge a flat fee and the technology improves your ability to deliver the services, and that technology cost can be passed on to the client. The impact can vary, but the constant should be alignment between the individual performance and the firm's objective to deliver value to its clients.

§ 8:5 Firm example: PERFORM REAL ESTATE

PERFORM REAL ESTATE is a two-partner firm with one associate and two paralegals plus an administrative assistant who occasionally bills. The PERFORM professionals practice real estate law, including transactions and litigation for commercial and residential matters. At this point, in numbers, there are more residential matters, but the commercial billings in dollars account for over three-quarters of the firm's annual revenue, approximately $1.5 million in billings.

Paul and Patty are the two partners and have worked together for about five years. They hired Allan as an associate attorney at the beginning of 2015. Allan has no client-development responsibilities. Both partners keep Larry and Louise, the two paralegals, extremely busy. Susan is the administrative assistant who is tasked with implementing new performance KPIs because the partners are trying to decide whether to hire another associate attorney or paralegal. Paul does larger commercial projects, and Patty spends more time on residential matters, but both do litigate.

The firm uses a time and billing system with an integrated calendar, as well as the QuickBooks accounting system (QuickBooks). PERFORM REAL ESTATE also has a website for triaging client inquiries and has no problem finding work. Patty is the rainmaker partner, while Paul is a billing machine, always hitting at least 100% utilization. The firm does not use flat fees but gives both their commercial and residential clients an estimate of the fees and number of hours. The commercial clients pay a retainer that is replenished, and most residential clients pay monthly based on billed hours. The firm occasionally has residential clients pay retainers for litigation but mostly allows their residential clients 30 days to pay.

When Susan first started five years ago, the firm was only the two partners and used the cash basis of accounting with just QuickBooks and no LPM. However, when they added the paralegals, they decided to move to a modified accrual accounting method to try to better match the costs with the revenue to stay on top of profitability. The firm employs an outside accountant that runs the bills on the last day of the month for the entire month.

Targets

Each year, Susan would prepare targets for the partners to review and approve in December. Last year, traditional utilization billable-hour targets were set in early December 2015 for 2016. The process was based on the partners' prior lives, where they worked an annual target rather than looking at what can actually be billed based on roles and responsibilities.

The partners and Susan meet in the last week of December to implement the new performance KPIs. To prepare, Susan provided the estimates below for the partners to review and adjust, given that the baseline annual available hours for PERFORM REAL ESTATE is 1,800 using the calculation above.

2016 Budgeted Billable Hours	Rate	Traditional Hours	Budgeted Revenue
Paul	$300	2,000	$600,000
Patty	$275	1,600	$440,000
Allan	$160	1,600	$256,000
Larry	$125	1,200	$150,000
Louise	$100	1,200	$120,000
Susan	$75	600	$45,000
TOTAL		8,200	$1,611,000

The partners decided to redo the hours by month based on schedules and assignment of targets based on time percentages. For example, Paul considers himself fully available for billable work. Despite Susan explaining that the baseline should be the 1,800 hours, Paul insists on still having a 2,000 annual available-hour amount. His logic is that he will do any other firm work over and above those 2,000 hours. Paul does concede to adjust the monthly targets for his planned vacations rather than just focusing on an annual target. Also, he has had some collection issues, so he applies a 1% discount.

Patty and Allan look at their workload, and Patty decides that she will spend 75% of her time actually practicing. As for the other attorney, Allan has no client-development responsibility but has to supervise the paralegals and Susan. The partners decide he will need to spend about 15% of his time on administrative time, including CLE.

§ 8:5

The partners feel that the paralegals should be 100% devoted to client work, and despite Susan's thoughts that they should have at least a few hours a month for administrative work and training, the partners decide that they should be at full capacity, or have 1,800 hours available for clients. Susan is able to convince the partners that she is at most one-third time in client work that can be billed. Both partners are not sure that they will be able to collect all of Susan's time at $75 per hour, so they add in a 5% discount.

Action: The partners agree to adopt the assumptions above and review the first quarter results, and Paul is interested in growing the firm's revenue to closer to $2 million in 2016. Patty would like to review all the rates after the first quarter and at year end. Susan will gather some information on the market rates which they then can compare to the KPI results. Paul would like to also continue to look at the traditional metrics for his practice, so they agree to continue to compile and review at year end.

§ 8:6 Firm example: PERFORM REAL ESTATE—First quarter results

5-PERF (a): Billings Collected by Attorney, 5-PERF (c): Net Collection by Attorney, and **Hourly Billings by Attorney** for the first three months of 2016:

PERFORM REAL ESTATE			
	Jan	Feb	Mar
Timekeeper	Billing Rate		
Paul	$300	$300	$300
5-PERF(a) Billings Collected by Attorney (%)	57%	42%	185%
TARGET—Billings Collected by Attorney (%)	99%	99%	99%
5-PERF(c) Net Collection by Attorney ($)	$176	$167	$625
TARGET—Net Collected by Attorney ($)	$297	$297	$297
5-PERF(e) Hourly Billings by Attorney ($)	$300	$300	$300
TARGET—Hourly Billings by Attorney ($)	$300	$300	$300

Deep Dive KPI 5: Performance (PERF) § 8:6

PERFORM REAL ESTATE			
	Jan	**Feb**	**Mar**
Timekeeper	Billing Rate		
5-PERF(g) Hourly Revenue Collected by Attorney ($)	NA	NA	$279
TARGET—Hourly Revenue Collected by Attorney ($)	NA	NA	?
Input—$ Collected by Timekeeper	$30,000	$25,000	$100,000
Input—$ Billed by Timekeeper	$52,500	$60,000	$54,000
Input—Available Hours by Timekeeper	170	150	160
Input—Actual Billed Hours by Timekeeper	175	200	180

Paul always runs an A/R balance because he bills out everything to his clients every month, but he does not have the clients on monthly retainers or even retainers for large projects. He started the year with a $30,000 A/R balance, and at the end of the first quarter it had grown to $41,500. In the first three months, Paul is billing a consistent amount and is above his available hours, but his collection is poor. Susan is concerned that the 5-PER(g) hourly revenue collected is running at $279 against an annual target of $300. Susan decides to try to convince Paul to start requesting retainers. She has also decided to look into collection software for the firm.

PERFORM REAL ESTATE			
	Jan	**Feb**	**Mar**
Timekeeper Name	Billing Rate		
Patty	$250	$250	$250
5-PERF(a) Billings Collected by Attorney (%)	129%	82%	82%
TARGET—Billings Collected by Attorney (%)	100%	100%	100%
5-PERF(c) Net Collection by Attorney ($)	$346	$173	$173
TARGET—Net Collected by Attorney ($)	$250	$250	$250

§ 8:6

PERFORM REAL ESTATE			
	Jan	**Feb**	**Mar**
Timekeeper Name	Billing Rate		
5-PERF(e) Hourly Billings by Attorney ($)	$250	$250	$250
TARGET—Hourly Billings by Attorney ($)	$250	$250	$250
5-PERF(g) Hourly Revenue Collected by Attorney ($)	NA	NA	$250
TARGET—Hourly Revenue Collected by Attorney ($)	NA	NA	?
Input—$ Collected by Timekeeper	$45,000	$22,500	$22,500
Input—$ Billed by Timekeeper	$35,000	$27,500	$27,500
Input—Available Hours by Timekeeper	130	130	130
Input—Actual Billed Hours by Timekeeper	140	110	110

Patty is thrilled with her first quarter results. After the meeting with Paul and Susan where they discussed how the KPIs work and that the focus is on cash collections, Patty had a separate meeting with Susan to discuss implementing retainers for all clients and has also put out two types of real estate project work that are based on a flat fee that clients would pay up front. Those matters would take two or three months. In January Patty receives $10,000 additional cash for one of those projects. The revenue is actually earned in February and March when the hours are billed by Patty. Patty records the hours and uses the earned-value method as explained in the profitability KPI chapter.

Susan's research shows that given Patty's experience and reputation, the local market can bear a rate increase to $275 per hour. Patty lets her clients know that, effective May 1st, she will be raising her rates and also offering the flat-fee approach to additional matters.

Deep Dive KPI 5: Performance (PERF) § 8:6

Timekeeper	Jan Billing Rate	Feb	Mar
Allan	$160	$160	$160
5-PERF(a) Billings Collected by Attorney (%)	88%	80%	75%
TARGET—Billings Collected by Attorney (%)	100%	100%	100%
5-PERF(c) Net Collection by Attorney ($)	$161	$147	$171
TARGET—Net Collected by Attorney ($)	$160	$160	$160
5-PERF(e) Hourly Billings by Attorney ($)	$160	$160	$160
TARGET—Hourly Billings by Attorney ($)	$160	$160	$160
5-PERF(g) Hourly Revenue Collected by Attorney ($) & (%)	NA	NA	$129
TARGET—Hourly Revenue Collected by Attorney ($)	NA	NA	?
Input—$ Collected by Timekeeper	$22,600	$20,600	$24,000
Input—$ Billed by Timekeeper	$25,600	$25,600	$32,000
Input—Available Hours by Timekeeper	140	140	140
Input—Actual Billed Hours by Timekeeper	160	160	200

Allan's results are not as impressive despite a great effort on his part. He splits his client time working on cases for Paul and Patty close to equally. Unfortunately, Allan only had the target from December as his goal and believes that the more he bills, the better his performance. He wishes to follow in Paul's footsteps and has been taking on more and more work. However, most simply put, it is quality over quantity in any business, and the law is no exception from the client's point of view.

Allan billed 520 hours versus his available hours of 420 in the first quarter. Paul explains that not only was he unable to collect all of the hours billed by Allan, but that Allan actually recorded 40 additional hours in unbilled time or WIP that was written off in the first quarter. Those 40 hours did not make it into the performance measures above but mean that Allan worked 560 hours on client matters, which, if that effort were annualized, would put him over 2,100 hours.

While Patty was careful to ensure that she only billed work that could be collected, Allan was busy racking up the hours on her matters also. The partners recognized that they needed to align Allan's performance goals with the firm goals and also provide better guidance. Allan's efforts needed to be refocused onto efficient delivery, and his compensation should be tied to his ability to hit the budgets and targets, not record as many hours as possible.

Action—Meeting with Allan to thank him for his efforts and explain the new model and goals as well as provide budgets for the tasks. This meeting should also include a discussion of how the paralegals could help Allan attain the dollar budgets because some of his research work was routine and would take the paralegals the same time at a lower billing rate.

However, the partners will explain that if Allan was unable to finish his tasks on budget, he should still record the time, but as non-billable to that client, so that all the time is recorded for pricing and future budgeting. Also, perhaps the work delegated to Allan is not appropriate or he needs additional training.

5-PERF (b): Billings Collected by Paralegal, 5-PERF (d): Net Collection by Paralegal, and **Hourly Billings by Paralegal** for the first three months of 2016:

PERFORM REAL ESTATE			
	Jan	**Feb**	**Mar**
Timekeeper Name	Billing Rate		
Larry	$125	$125	$125
5-PERF(b) Billings Collected by Paralegal (%)	100%	100%	100%
TARGET—Billings Collected by Paralegal (%)	100%	100%	100%
5-PERF(d) Net Collection by Paralegal ($)	$100	$113	$94
TARGET—Net Collected by Paralegal ($)	$125	$125	$125
5-PERF(f) Hourly Billings by Paralegal ($)	$125	$125	$125
TARGET—Hourly Billings by Paralegal ($)	$125	$125	$125

DEEP DIVE KPI 5: PERFORMANCE (PERF) § 8:6

PERFORM REAL ESTATE			
	Jan	**Feb**	**Mar**
Timekeeper Name	Billing Rate		
5-PERF(h) Hourly Revenue Collected by Paralegal ($) & (%)	NA	NA	$125
TARGET—Hourly Revenue Collected by Paralegal ($)	NA	NA	?
Input—$ Collected by Timekeeper	$15,000	$16,875	$15,000
Input—$ Billed by Timekeeper	$15,000	$16,875	$15,000
Input—Available Hours by Timekeeper	150	150	160
Input—Actual Billed Hours by Timekeeper	120	135	120

PERFORM REAL ESTATE			
	Jan	**Feb**	**Mar**
Timekeeper Name	Billing Rate		
Louise	$100	$100	$100
5-PERF(b) Billings Collected by Paralegal (%)	100%	100%	100%
TARGET—Billings Collected by Paralegal (%)	100%	100%	100%
5-PERF(d) Net Collection by Paralegal ($)	$80	$90	$75
TARGET—Net Collected by Paralegal ($)	$100	$100	$100
5-PERF(f) Hourly Billings by Paralegal ($)	$100	$100	$100
TARGET—Hourly Billings by Paralegal ($)	$100	$100	$100
5-PERF(h) Hourly Revenue Collected by Paralegal ($) & (%)	NA	NA	$100
TARGET—Hourly Revenue Collected by Paralegal ($)	NA	NA	?

PERFORM REAL ESTATE			
	Jan	Feb	Mar
Timekeeper Name	Billing Rate		
Input—$ Collected by Timekeeper	$12,000	$13,500	$12,000
Input—$ Billed by Timekeeper	$12,000	$13,500	$12,000
Input—Available Hours by Timekeeper	150	150	160
Input—Actual Billed Hours by Timekeeper	120	135	120

Like Allan was not in the loop, Susan had not told the paralegals Larry and Louise that their targets had been changed because she thought that the partners would be meeting with them to discuss in January. When Susan and the partners reviewed these first quarter results, they agreed to set up a meeting with everyone.

The paralegals are working hard, and everything recorded and billed is being collected; it is just that they are falling short of the partner's expectations that have not been communicated.

The partners discuss the paralegals' billing rates and agree to change Louise's rate to match that of Larry's $125 because the partners agree that their skill set and experience is the same. At the end of the year, they will review Louise's 5-PERF(g) hourly revenue collected KPI along with the same for Larry to see if the rate change makes sense.

Action—Susan will organize a team meeting for all timekeepers in April to review the performance metrics, and the partners will discuss Allan's supervision of the paralegals with him prior to the meeting. Available-hour assumptions and vacations will be double checked.

PERFORM REAL ESTATE			
	Jan	Feb	Mar
Susan	$75	$75	$75
5-PERF(b)Billings Collected by Admin (%)	100%	100%	100%
TARGET—Billings Collected by Admin (%)	95%	95%	95%
5-PERF(d) Net Collection by Admin ($)	$38	$90	$113

Deep Dive KPI 5: Performance (PERF) § 8:6

PERFORM REAL ESTATE			
	Jan	**Feb**	**Mar**
TARGET—Net Collected by Admin ($)	$71	$71	$71
5-PERF(f) Hourly Billings by Admin ($)	**$75**	**$75**	**$75**
TARGET—Hourly Billings by Admin ($)	$75	$75	$75
5-PERF(h) Hourly Revenue Collected by Admin ($) & (%)	NA	NA	$75
TARGET—Hourly Revenue Collected by Admin ($)	NA	NA	?
Input—$ Collected by Timekeeper	$1,875	$4,500	$5,625
Input—$ Billed by Timekeeper	$1,875	$4,500	$5,625
Input—Available Hours by Timekeeper	50	50	50
Input—Actual Billed Hours by Timekeeper	25	60	75

Susan really felt like her legal support skill set had been unutilized. She has been with the two partners for years and knows how to do many of the paralegal research tasks; she is solely responsible for the report preparation and the logistics for the trial in addition to preparing any exhibits. She asks the partners to consider a rate increase for 2017 and also an expanded target because she believes that the client deserves the best value and that paying a paralegal to do simple administration and filing of documents is not good business. Paul and Patty are intrigued by Susan's ideas about how to deliver the same product for less to clients. Luckily Paul sees the bigger picture that they can hire additional paralegals or attorneys for the higher level work.

§ 8:6

5-PERF (g): Hourly Revenue Collected by Attorney and **5-PERF (h): Hourly Revenue Collected by Paralegal** will be normally be calculated annually, but Susan ran the data for the first three months for attorneys and paralegals, and it is included above and used below around pricing and rates.

§ 8:7 Firm example: PERFORM REAL ESTATE—Full year results

The full year results are included in Exhibit 1 at the end of the chapter. Below are the overall individual performance results. Paul's information will be examined in depth to demonstrate the additional information that is uncovered by going beyond a traditional utilization measurement, and one additional optional annual KPI percentage will be added to each timekeeper under 5-PERF(g) and (h), revenues collected. The latter uses the data already captured and is just another simple calculation.

Paul was curious about how his year looked under the traditional metrics:

2016 Traditional Utilization	Rate	Traditional Hours	Actual Billed	Utilization
Paul	$300	2,000	2,135	107%

Under these traditional metrics, Paul would be considered a high performer because he is at 107% utilization. However, he may have billed 2,135 hours at $300 per hour or $640,500, which was $40,500 more than his target or budgeted revenue of $600,000, but he did not collect all of it. Instead his collections within 2016 were $598,000, and $30,000 of that was from 2015 work that was not collected until March 2016. Thus his actual collections were $568,000, and during the year, he wrote off $32,500 on a client matter in June for work done over a couple of months, as the client was unhappy. That included $10,000 of Allan's time, so the impact on Paul's individual performance data was $22,500.

There was also a time-lag issue because some of that $598,000 was collected for work done in 2015, and some of the $640,500 will be collected in 2017. Paul started the year with $30,000 in A/R and ended the year with $50,000.

Deep Dive KPI 5: Performance (PERF) § 8:7

Cash flow is reconciled as follows:

Cash collections within 2016	$598,000
Remove 2015 collections	($30,000)
Cash collected for 2016 work	$568,000
Ending A/R balance	$50,000
Total potentially collectable for 2016	$618,000
Add back the write-off	$22,500
Total billings for 2016	**$640,500**

Depending on the difference between opening and ending A/R balances, the 5-PERF(g) and (h) Hourly Revenues Collected KPIs can vary by timekeeper. Exhibit 1 assumes that the balances do not materially impact the results and leaves in the $30K that was collected in 2016 for 2015 work. The concept is that there will be work that is billed in 2016 that is not yet collected to offset the $30,000.

The $50,000 included in ending A/R is also included in revenue for the financial statements but theoretically should not be in the KPI. This is because firms do not adjust for the net difference between opening and closing A/R, and at this point there is no certainty that it will be collected. Below are the recalculated ratios adjusting for the impact of the A/R that show how much Paul realized for each hour on client work.

Original	Without 2015 $
$598K	$568K
2,135 hours	2,135 hours
=$280	=$266

There is another way to look at the dollars, and in some cases, also the hours that were written off as uncollectible within the period. In this case Paul wrote off $22,500 of time during the year because he could not collect that money. Therefore, it is not really important that the utilization is over 100%; rather, the goal is to collect everything that is billed.

Also using the same data and comparing collected dollars to billed dollars under 5-PERF(a), the billings collected or collection realization percentage can be calculated as it was in Exhibit 1.

§ 8:7   LAW FIRM KEY PERFORMANCE INDICATORS

The prior years' $30,000 cash collection can then also be removed.

Original	Without 2015 $
$598,000	$568,000
$640,500	$640,500
= 93%	= 89%

Paul's realized or collected billings as a percentage are somewhere between 89% and 93% of the amount billed. The 93% is the 5-PERF (a) Billings Collected by Attorney KPI in the annual column because the KPIs do not adjust for the A/R timing differences.

This is an area to explore further for billing rates and revenue budgets. It is not necessary to go through these timing differences for everyone in the firm, but it is something to review at the end of each year to see if there are significant variations in A/R and material write-offs. Also, it is good practice to look at the WIP lockup days under the third KPI, profitability, 3-PROF(g) in conjunction with the performance KPI.

In 2016, the revenue target was exceeded, as is seen below. Overall the rate increases and the additional hours led to billings of $1,849,600 against a budget of $1,611,000. However, the important figure was the collections of $1,752,000. At the firm level there was a Billings Collected by Timekeeper or collection realization percentage of 94.7%.

2016 Budgeted vs. Billings	Budgeted Revenue	Billings
Paul	$600,000	$640,500
Patty	$440,000	$447,875
Allan	$256,000	$297,600
Larry	$150,000	$206,875
Louise	$120,000	$211,750
Susan	$45,000	$45,000
TOTAL	**$1,611,000**	**$1,849,600**

If instead utilization rates for the timekeepers are scrutinized using the original traditional hour targets set in December 2015, it shows only part of the story. If the partners had only looked at utilization, perhaps that may have driven some different changes without the full KPIs per timekeeper in Exhibit 1. See below for the wide difference in the results.

Deep Dive KPI 5: Performance (PERF) § 8:7

The challenges with collection or realization of the rates was picked up by analyzing not just utilization but the 5-PERF (a) Billings and (c) Collection for Attorneys along with 5-PERF (b) Billings and (d) Collections for Paralegals and Susan.

2016 Billings Collected vs. Utilization	Billings Collected	Utilization
Paul	93.36%	106.75%
Patty	100.00%	104.56%
Allan	86.22%	116.25%
Larry	96.13%	137.92%
Louise	97.17%	150.00%
Susan	100.00%	60.00%

Timekeeper highlights

Paul's data was analyzed above, but in a nutshell, he realized that generating billable hours should not be his focus. He needs to continue to work with Allan and the paralegals around creating budgets and staying on budget for hours that will be charged to the clients. He did speak to Patty and Susan about their results to see what tactics can be used to raise his 5-PERF KPI results. He is very interested in the retainers and monthly fees.

Patty continued 2016 with her new billing rate of $275 versus $250 and maintained a 100% 5-PERF(a) Billings Collected by Attorney KPI result for the collection realization percentage for her work. However, Allan and the paralegals continued to struggle with trying to maximize billable hours and adhere to budgets.

Allan exceeded his budgeted revenue by more than $40,000, or about 15%; however, the actual cash collected was closer to the budgeted $256,000. Allan ended up with the $10,000 write-off from Paul's client and then several from Patty, totaling about $30,000 more. Allan in particular finished the year with an 86% 5-PERF billings collection. However, in the last four months, things improved, and overall from the first quarter to the annual results Allan's hourly revenue collected has steadily improved.

The partners noticed that in about three areas, Allan's billings were consistently over budget, and they had to sit down with him in the early fall to explain that they would be revisiting the firm budgets for those clients. However, as the clients had been given budgets at lower amounts, they had to write off some of his billings. They did reassure him that it was a firm budgeting issue and did not impact his compensation. Allan now understands that it is not about the number of absolute hours but instead the hours that will ultimately be collectible.

Larry and Louise did pick up the pace in terms of billed hours once they understood the revised targets. Importantly, both had hourly revenue KPIs that were very close to their billing rates, and the 5-PERF (b) Billings Collected results improved and were closer to 100%. Larry seemed extremely busy all year and was surprised that he was not at 100%. The partners explained the same issues that impacted Allan's results had reduced their collections, albeit to a lesser extent. Larry was ill in December, and Louise had picked up his workload, which explained the anomalies there.

Susan's results were excellent, but Patty questioned whether she was actually billing all the time that she was spending, as she billed precisely her target of 600 hours. Susan did admit that she did not want to fall into the same category as Allan and bill more than could be collected. However, Patty was concerned that the tasks were not properly budgeted. She and Susan discuss having nonbillable time codes for all client matters that can be used for budgeting purposes without messing up the actual billings. Also, both partners need to plan their matters with the appropriate budget for the appropriate level. If Susan is doing a task, it will take her longer than Allan, for example.

Changes

Increased billing rates—Patty and Louise changed their rates, and it did not have an adverse effect on collection. Susan and Allan's rates will be reviewed in the first quarter of 2017.

Amend available hours and targets—Paul and Patty commit to proposing available hours and targets for all the performance KPIs that are vetted and reviewed by the team before the year starts.

Retainers for large projects, evergreen wherever possible—With a couple of years of data, Paul will adopt Patty's retainer approach and also develop budgets for the matters. Paul commits to developing detailed budgets with the different tasks assigned to various timekeepers.

Fixed fees for smaller matters—Patty has some smaller routine transactional matters that she believes that Allan can handle. Also, she is researching the use of technology: Fewer hours, more delivery—use technology.

Client development responsibilities—Later in 2017, Patty will train Allan to do some client development because his rate is lower and some of those smaller matters can be prospected and won by Allan. This will free Patty up to do more client work.

Deep Dive KPI 5: Performance (PERF) § 8:7

New hire decisions—Although the KPIs informed the partners as to the issues, they feel that they need a few more months to decide whether the next hire is an attorney or paralegal.

Rolling targets—The targets will be set for all of 2017, but they agree to revisit each quarter.

They all agreed that 2016 was a learning year and part of a process to align the individual performance measures with the firm goals and path forward.

Fees vs. hours

The KPIs for Billings Collected by Timekeeper (5-PERF(a) and (b)) work for firms that are no longer using hourly rates to bill clients because hours are not in the calculation. However, you can still calculate the performance metrics with recorded hours in place of billed hours for the KPIs 5-PERF(c) to (h). As discussed above, it is critical to continue to record hours on matters regardless of fee structure.

Also, if your time and billing system does not show collections by timekeeper, then you can examine where the write-offs occur at the matter level. Firms should start with the high-level results for the firm, finding the matters where the collection is less than the billing, and then work down to timekeeper.

Pricing

Rates or fees must be set at what the market can bear. However, the 5-PROF(g) WIP and (h) A/R KPI, Hourly Revenue Collected by Attorney and Paralegal, provide excellent price point information. Also, comparing the 5-PROF (a) ROI and 5-PROF (b) Contribution Margin shows the difference between billing and collection, or a realization rate. By analyzing the budgeted rates versus the hourly revenue collected, informed hourly rate pricing decisions can be made. For flat fees or monthly retainers, a review of the budgeted versus actual effort plus the cost of any technology must be added to the information below.

2016 Budgeted vs. Billings	Budgeted Rates	Hourly Revenue Collected
Paul	$300	$280
Patty (revised to $275 May 2016)	$250	$268
Allan	$160	$138
Larry	$125	$120
Louise (revised to $125 April 2016)	$100	$114
Susan	$75	$75

Deep Dive KPI 5: Performance (PERF) § 8:7

Exhibit 1—Performance PERFORM REAL ESTATE 2016

PERFORM REAL ESTATE — Timekeeper: Paul

	Billing Rate	Jan	Feb	Mar	Apr	May	June	July	Aug	Sept	Oct	Nov	Dec	ANNUAL
5-PERF(q) Billings Collected by Attorney (%)		57%	42%	185%	143%	92%	42%	37%	222%	108%	60%	92%	133%	93%
TARGET - Billings Collected by Attorney (%)		100%	99%	99%	99%	99%	99%	99%	99%	99%	99%	99%	99%	99%
5-PERF(c) Net Collection by Attorney ($)		$176	$167	$625	$443	$275	$125	$110	$800	$336	$185	$314	$411	$299
TARGET - Net Collected by Attorney ($)		$297	$297	$297	$297	$297	$297	$297	$297	$297	$297	$297	$297	$297
5-PERF(e) Hourly Billings by Attorney ($)	$300	$300	$300	$300	$300	$300	$300	$300	$300	$300	$300	$300	$300	$300
TARGET - Hourly Billings by Attorney ($)		$300	$300	$300	$300	$300	$300	$300	$300	$300	$300	$300	$300	$300
5-PERF(g) Hourly Revenue Collected by Attorney ($)				$279									$280	
TARGET - Hourly Revenue Collected by Attorney ($)				?									$300	
Input - $ collected by timekeeper		$30,000	$25,000	$100,000	$75,000	$55,000	$25,000	$22,000	$60,000	$42,000	$37,000	$55,000	$72,000	$598,000
Input - $ billed by timekeeper		$52,500	$60,000	$54,000	$52,500	$60,000	$60,000	$60,000	$27,000	$39,000	$61,500	$60,000	$54,000	$640,500
Input - available hours by timekeeper		170	160	180	175	200	200	200	75	125	200	175	175	2000
Input - actual billed hours by timekeeper		175	200	180	175	200	200	200	90	130	205	200	180	2135

PERFORM REAL ESTATE — Timekeeper: Patty

	Billing Rate	Jan	Feb	Mar	Apr	May	June	July	Aug	Sept	Oct	Nov	Dec	ANNUAL
5-PERF(q) Billings Collected by Attorney (%)		129%	82%	82%	100%	100%	134%	76%	77%	50%	146%	100%	100%	100%
TARGET - Billings Collected by Attorney (%)		100%	100%	100%	100%	100%	100%	100%	100%	100%	100%	100%	100%	100%
5-PERF(c) Net Collection by Attorney ($)		$346	$173	$173	$246	$338	$382	$240	$160	$152	$438	$344	$344	$260
TARGET - Net Collected by Attorney ($)		$250	$250	$250	$250	$250	$250	$250	$250	$250	$250	$250	$250	$250
5-PERF(e) Hourly Billings by Attorney ($)	$250	$275	$275	$275	$275	$275	$275	$275	$275	$275	$275	$275	$275	$268
TARGET - Hourly Billings by Attorney ($)		$250	$250	$250	$250	$250	$250	$250	$250	$250	$250	$250	$250	$250
5-PERF(g) Hourly Revenue Collected by Attorney ($)				$250									$268	
TARGET - Hourly Revenue Collected by Attorney ($)				?									$250	
Input - $ collected by timekeeper		$45,000	$22,500	$22,500	$32,000	$44,000	$47,750	$15,625	$23,250	$22,000	$70,125	$48,125	$55,000	$447,875
Input - $ billed by timekeeper		$35,000	$27,500	$27,500	$32,000	$44,000	$35,750	$20,625	$30,250	$44,000	$48,125	$48,125	$55,000	$447,875
Input - available hours by timekeeper		140	110	130	130	160	130	65	145	145	140	150	200	1600
Input - actual billed hours by timekeeper		140	110	110	128	160	130	75	110	160	175	175	200	1673

PERFORM REAL ESTATE — Timekeeper: Allan

	Billing Rate	Jan	Feb	Mar	Apr	May	June	July	Aug	Sept	Oct	Nov	Dec	ANNUAL
5-PERF(q) Billings Collected by Attorney (%)		88%	80%	75%	64%	92%	55%	101%	88%	100%	114%	94%	98%	86%
TARGET - Billings Collected by Attorney (%)		100%	100%	100%	100%	100%	100%	100%	100%	100%	100%	100%	100%	100%
5-PERF(c) Net Collection by Attorney ($)		$161	$147	$171	$147	$99	$161	$565	$114	$183	$192	$153	$268	
TARGET - Net Collected by Attorney ($)		$160	$160	$160	$160	$160	$160	$160	$160	$160	$160	$160	$160	$160
5-PERF(e) Hourly Billings by Attorney ($)	$160	$160	$160	$160	$160	$160	$160	$160	$160	$160	$160	$160	$160	$160
TARGET - Hourly Billings by Attorney ($)		$160	$160	$160	$160	$160	$160	$160	$160	$160	$160	$160	$160	$160
5-PERF(g) Hourly Revenue Collected by Attorney ($)				$129									$138	
TARGET - Hourly Revenue Collected by Attorney ($)				?									$160	
Input - $ collected by timekeeper		$22,600	$20,600	$24,000	$20,600	$20,600	$12,400	$22,600	$22,600	$16,000	$25,600	$24,000	$25,000	$256,600
Input - $ billed by timekeeper		$25,600	$25,600	$32,500	$32,000	$22,400	$22,400	$22,400	$25,600	$25,600	$22,400	$25,000	$25,000	$297,600
Input - available hours by timekeeper		140	140	140	140	140	140	140	40	140	140	180	130	1530
Input - actual billed hours by timekeeper		160	160	200	200	140	140	140	160	100	140	160	160	1850

§ 8:7 LAW FIRM KEY PERFORMANCE INDICATORS

PERFORM REAL ESTATE	Jan	Feb	Mar	Apr	May	June	July	Aug	Sept	Oct	Nov	Dec	ANNUAL
Timekeeper Name	Billing Rate												
Larry	$125	$125	$125	$125	$125	$125	$125	$125	$125	$125	$125	$125	
$-PERF(a) Billings Collected by Paralegal (%)	100%	100%	100%	100%	100%	100%	100%	70%	100%	84%	100%	100%	96%
TARGET - Billings Collected by Paralegal (%)	100%	100%	100%	100%	100%	100%	100%	100%	100%	100%	100%	100%	100%
$-PERF(c) Net Collection by Paralegal ($)	$100	$113	$94	$121	$121	$172	$182	$79	$121	$98	$109	$47	$110
TARGET - Net Collected by Paralegal ($)	$125	$125	$125	$125	$125	$125	$125	$125	$125	$125	$125	$125	$125
$-PERF(e) Hourly Billings by Paralegal ($)	$125	$125	$125	$125	$125	$125	$125	$125	$125	$125	$125	$125	$125
TARGET - Hourly Billings by Paralegal ($)	$125	$125	$125	$125	$125	$125	$125	$125	$125	$125	$125	$125	$125
$-PERF(g) Hourly Revenue Collected by Paralegal ($)			$125									$120	
			?									$125	
Input - $collected by timekeeper	$15,000	$16,875	$15,000	$19,375	$19,375	$20,625	$21,875	$11,875	$18,125	$15,750	$17,500	$7,500	$198,875
Input - $billed by timekeeper	$15,000	$16,875	$15,000	$19,375	$19,375	$20,625	$21,875	$16,875	$18,125	$18,750	$17,500	$7,500	$206,875
Input - available hours by timekeeper	150	150	160	160	160	120	150	150	150	150	160	160	1800
Input - actual billed hours by timekeeper	120	135	120	155	155	165	175	135	145	150	140	60	1655

PERFORM REAL ESTATE	Jan	Feb	Mar	Apr	May	June	July	Aug	Sept	Oct	Nov	Dec	ANNUAL
Timekeeper Name	Billing Rate												
Louise	$100	$100	$100	$100	$125	$125	$125	$125	$125	$125	$125	$125	
$-PERF(a) Billings Collected by Paralegal (%)	100%	100%	100%	100%	100%	100%	100%	100%	100%	100%	85%	87%	97%
TARGET - Billings Collected by Paralegal (%)	100%	100%	100%	100%	100%	100%	100%	100%	100%	100%	100%	100%	100%
$-PERF(c) Net Collection by Paralegal ($)	$80	$90	$75	$97	$121	$138	$146	$141	$151	$117	$106	$126	$114
TARGET - Net Collected by Paralegal ($)	$100	$100	$100	$100	$125	$125	$125	$125	$125	$125	$125	$125	$125
$-PERF(e) Hourly Billings by Paralegal ($)	$100	$100	$100	$100	$125	$125	$125	$125	$125	$125	$125	$125	$118
TARGET - Hourly Billings by Paralegal ($)	$100	$100	$100	$100	$125	$125	$125	$125	$125	$125	$125	$125	$125
$-PERF(g) Hourly Revenue Collected by Paralegal ($)			$100									$114	
			?									$100	
Input - $collected by timekeeper	$12,000	$13,500	$12,000	$15,500	$19,375	$20,625	$21,875	$16,875	$18,125	$18,750	$17,000	$20,125	$205,750
Input - $billed by timekeeper	$12,000	$13,500	$12,000	$15,500	$19,375	$20,625	$21,875	$16,875	$18,125	$18,750	$20,000	$23,125	$211,750
Input - available hours by timekeeper	150	150	160	160	160	150	150	120	120	160	160	160	1800
Input - actual billed hours by timekeeper	120	135	120	155	155	165	175	135	145	150	160	185	1800

PERFORM REAL ESTATE	Jan	Feb	Mar	Apr	May	June	July	Aug	Sept	Oct	Nov	Dec	ANNUAL
Timekeeper Name	Billing Rate												
Susan	$75	$75	$75	$75	$75	$75	$75	$75	$75	$75	$75	$75	
$-PERF(a) Billings Collected by Admin (%)	100%	100%	100%	100%	100%	100%	100%	100%	100%	100%	100%	100%	100%
TARGET - Billings Collected by Admin (%)	95%	95%	95%	95%	95%	95%	95%	95%	95%	95%	95%	95%	95%
$-PERF(c) Net Collection by Admin ($)	$38	$90	$113	$75	$75	$90	$38	$38	$113	$60	$68	$105	$71
TARGET - Net Collected by Admin ($)	$71	$71	$71	$71	$71	$71	$71	$71	$71	$71	$71	$71	$71
$-PERF(e) Hourly Billings by Admin ($)	$75	$75	$75	$75	$75	$75	$75	$75	$75	$75	$75	$75	$75
TARGET - Hourly Billings by Admin ($)	$75	$75	$75	$75	$75	$75	$75	$75	$75	$75	$75	$75	$75
$-PERF(g) Hourly Revenue Collected by Admin ($)			$75										
			?										
Input - $collected by timekeeper	$1,875	$4,500	$5,625	$3,750	$3,750	$4,500	$1,875	$1,875	$5,625	$3,000	$3,375	$5,250	$45,000
Input - $billed by timekeeper	$1,875	$4,500	$5,625	$3,750	$3,750	$4,500	$1,875	$1,875	$5,625	$3,000	$3,375	$5,250	$45,000
Input - available hours by timekeeper	50	50	50	50	50	50	50	50	50	50	50	50	600
Input - actual billed hours by timekeeper	25	60	75	50	50	60	25	25	75	40	45	70	600

§ 8:8 Firm example: PERFORM REAL ESTATE—Prior year data points

With some of the results above, Susan decides to pull the data to create a 2014 and 2015 baseline. She will not have targets, but that data can inform setting targets and other additional changes for 2017. Susan just reuses the Excel sheet from 2016 and creates new sheets with the same formulas. In the two prior years, the firm tracked traditional utilization, so Susan includes that in the results similar to 2016.

When she runs the numbers, Patty's stats have improved over time, while Paul's have not. The retainers and flat fees are helping Patty. Paul did collect retainers back in 2014 but has never charged flat fees. Susan did a bit more research and drilled into some of Paul's bigger matters in the past two years. During the times when Paul created a retainer and budget for large projects, there were better collection results.

Unfortunately, Allan only started at the beginning of 2015, and like any new attorney, the first few months were in training, and, therefore, most of the data is not helpful. The paralegal information seems quite static, and the trends match the partners on the matters.

§ 8:9 Technology to assist with performance KPIs

Properly implemented, technology can not only assist with data collection and reduce duplication of tasks, but also improve and streamline law firm workflow or process. Some of the technology that can be used to assist with Performance KPIs include:

- Excel—To avoid problems with various versions of the same spreadsheet, use a safe shared drive or server and create links between different workbooks and sheets to simplify data input. If you can regularly export an Excel or csv file from your time and billing system, accounting, or LPM, you can then link that file to your KPI spreadsheet to avoid duplicate data entry.
- Accounting Software—As accounting for legal services is more complex than the average small business, an accounting system that handles retainers, trust accounting, and modified accrual method may be necessary.
- Time and Billing Software—Again, due to the billing complexities and modified accounting methods, time and billing software is often necessary. If a firm is using multiple systems, interoperability is important. The LPM, accounting system, and time and billing must integrate to provide consistent data.

- Collections Software—Any type of software that can automate the follow up on invoices outstanding for more than certain number of days should improve collection rates.

A nonexhaustive list of technology resources is in APPENDIX D.

§ 8:10 Common mistakes or pitfalls

The above firm example and other experiences give rise to lessons learned that are set out below as common mistakes or pitfalls to avoid:

- Being reactive. Either gather a year's worth of go forward data or go back a year if you have readily accessible information to calculate these performance KPIs at the individual level. Once you have the trends, then check your assumptions regarding available hours and client collections before making any radical changes to billing rates or fees.
- Discarding these KPIs if you have flat fees. Utilization is still simple to calculate, even if you have flat fees because you should still be recording the hours on client work. If you do not have hours, you can amend the calculations to be based all on dollars billed and collected. However, recording hours is critical to pricing information.
- Encountering timing issues. These can be avoided with a good understanding of not only the accounting method but the business process and cash flow of the firm. Also, running a prior year for a couple of attorneys can often show whether it is okay to just use the data as is, set up a time lag, or measure on a quarterly or annual basis.
- Ignoring detailed budgets. Many firms set a target revenue or prepared a budget based on the billable-hour target multiplied by the billing rates. Unless your clients have unlimited funds and are not price sensitive, budgets should be set internally using a zero-based method for fees as well as costs. These budgets can be used to provide estimates to clients or build the basis for flat fees.
- Working top down or not communicating. Imposing targets without discussions and vetting of the assumptions is counterproductive. Examples of this would be not looking at people's circumstances or not requesting simple input, such as asking for information on vacation timing.

Next it is necessary to shift gears and measure the client experience with a firm. Formal KPIs in this area will be new to many firms, and again, firms should start small and build upon their metrics.

Chapter 9

Deep Dive KPI 6: Client Experience (CE)

§ 9:1   Introduction
§ 9:2   KPI 6—Client experience (CE) summary
§ 9:3   Data and sources
§ 9:4   Background
§ 9:5   Firm example: CE BUSINESS
§ 9:6   —First quarter results
§ 9:7   —Full year results
§ 9:8   —Prior year data points
§ 9:9   Technology to assist with client experience KPIs
§ 9:10 Common mistakes or pitfalls

§ 9:1 Introduction

Arguably the client experience (CE) KPI belongs at the top of the list of KPIs because without clients, there is no need for lawyers. However, this KPI framework is presented as a workflow in an order that follows first finding a prospective new client, securing and serving that client, and finally obtaining feedback from the client and within the firm when applicable. Thus, although it is the sixth step in the typical workflow, it is critical to the long-term viability of the firm.

As mentioned previously, it is easier to upsell or obtain more work from existing clients than find and develop brand new clients. The best indicator of repeat work or referrals is client satisfaction. Although it is not necessary to wait until the end of the engagement to ask for feedback, you should never complete an assignment without requesting feedback.

§ 9:2 KPI 6—Client experience (CE) summary

The sixth KPI area on Client Experience (CE) contains three metrics, as outlined in the table below, and APPENDIX B, Comprehensive KPI Listing—KPI 6: Client Experience, presents the information in table format with formulas.

§ 9:2   LAW FIRM KEY PERFORMANCE INDICATORS

6-CE Metrics	Calculation	Frequency*
6-CE (a): Net Promoter Score (NPS) (%)	The percentage of total clients responding to the survey question who are promoters less the percentage of total clients responding who are detractors	Monthly
6-CE (b): Client Services Recovery Rate (%)	The number of clients responding to the survey question who move from detractor or neutral to promoter divided by the total number of clients responding who were detractors or neutral	Quarterly
6-CE (c): Bar Complaints (#)	The number of complaints filed with the state bar	Monthly

* We recommend that KPIs are tracked regularly, either monthly, quarterly, or annually, once fully implemented. In the early stages of adoption, try to collect as much data as possible monthly and do an assessment at the end of the first quarter, including a comparison to the prior year. Some metrics will lend themselves to monthly measurement, while others will be naturally quarterly or annually. However, each firm's situation will be different, and there is simply no right or wrong approach to measurement; therefore, the frequencies listed in the table are only recommendations or examples.

§ 9:3 Data and sources

In most cases, legal client feedback has not been formalized into a survey format or process. Many attorneys ask clients for referrals, provide cards for their friends and family, and use other, informal methods to gauge their success with clients. Using the NPS approach or methodology is actually borrowing from consumer-facing companies and software as a service. Therefore, it is unlikely that there will be prior year data from any other source that will allow for the measurement of 6-CE(a) NPS or (b) Client Service Recovery Rate.

The source for 6-CE(a) NPS will be a simple survey that can be done using online software platforms like Survey Monkey or Google Docs. We recommend that if end of engagement letters are sent electronically, that the link to the survey be included in the letter or the e-mail. Also, the survey can be added into the invoicing process. Some firms even have an administrator call and ask the two questions below over the phone and record the answers in a log or Excel worksheet.

Client lists come from either the accounting system, the legal practice management (LPM) system, or the customer relationship management (CRM) system, wherever the electronic rolodex exists. That said, the survey can be verbal or done with a letter, and a LPM and CRM are not requirements.

NPS Questions—The standard question to be asked of clients is: "On a scale of one to 10 (with one being not at all likely and 10 being extremely likely), how likely are they to recommend your firm to their friends, family, and colleagues?" The goal is to be scored as a 9 or 10 because then that client is a promoter. They are likely to refer clients to you based on their positive experience.

Depending on the type of firm, the "friends, family, and colleagues" can be tailored to be as simple as "others"; "other companies"; or "others seeking a <type of practice> lawyer."

It is a good idea, particularly early on, to also ask a second NPS question to immediately follow the first: "Why, or Why Not?" The answers will need to be recorded by client; anonymous information will not allow you to follow up with additional questions or clarifications, or to resurvey.

For the 6-CE(b) Client Services Recovery Rate, we send another survey to only detractors and neutrals. In order to resurvey those who responded as non-promoters or neutrals or detractors, we need to know who responded with what number in the original survey. We then send out a follow-up survey only if we have continued to work for that client either on an ongoing basis or for a new project. It would be prudent to wait for at least several months to resurvey.

Bar Complaints—For the 6-CE(c) Bar Complaints, we are interested in the number of complaints filed with the Bar, not only those that result in any discipline. Knowing the number filed is important because it may indicate trends with certain practice areas or particular attorneys. Of course, the impact from bar complaints that result in sanctions or suspensions on the firm reputation is something that can damage the brand.

§ 9:4 Background

Although measuring client experience is a relatively new concept in the legal profession, knowing what you can improve upon based feedback is critical to any business. As mentioned, service and software businesses have been using client feedback metrics for years. Many of you will have received an email with one or two questions on your experience using a software platform, shopping online, or visiting a hotel. If your firm has consumers as clients, they will also be familiar with the NPS question.

Consumers are used to being able to give feedback now with platforms like Yelp and comment sections on blogs and websites. Lawyers should not fear the feedback because it is the best way to know what you are doing well and what needs improvement.

However, asking your clients how likely are they are to recommend your firm to their friends, family, and colleagues is only useful if you are willing to evaluate the results. Also you must be prepared to address the answers to the follow-on why or why not question. Asking for feedback without the intention of taking corrective action will frustrate your clients and staff alike.

NPS scoring is a widely known metric and can be used to promote your firm on your website or in marketing material, whether you are a solo or a firm with 30 lawyers. In fact, big law firms are now implementing these NPS questions as part of their metrics.

Finally, the bar complaints need to be managed, as it is your or your firm's reputation at stake. With more and more information available to the public online, potential clients will search your name and your firm's name online.

§ 9:5 Firm example: CE BUSINESS

BUSINESS is a firm specializing in all types of business matters, including bankruptcy and commercial litigation. Formed 20 years ago, BUSINESS works with start-ups to established local corporations. They do not work with consumers, other than those who are starting a new business for the first time.

The managing partner, Clint Chester, is intrigued by an article that he read about one of his business clients and their use of the net promoter score (NPS). After discussing it with the other four partners, they decide to investigate the client experience KPIs with the assistance of the office manager, Edith Espinosa.

BUSINESS has a website that allows clients to call and schedule an appointment or fill in a contact form. All five partners are active speakers, and two of them teach as adjuncts at a local law school. The firm has a total of 20 attorneys plus six paralegals and four legal assistants. Clint and the partners pride themselves on being forward thinking and are enthusiastic technology users.

About three years ago, Clint invested in a customer relationship management (CRM) system that is integrated with the firm's

Deep Dive KPI 6: Client Experience (CE) § 9:5

cloud-based legal practice management (LPM) system and the website. He and the partners have worked hard to implement a client-development culture. All the attorneys use the system to log in prospective clients, and the firm does a monthly newsletter for their mailing list in addition to the blog on their website. Edith runs a monthly report with analytics such as visitors and their time on the site.

BUSINESS also is piloting a flat monthly fee for start-ups to access unlimited legal resources in addition to their project flat fees and regular, time-based fees for other matters. Some of the financing transactions or deals for client acquisitions are done on a time basis not to exceed a certain amount.

Clint is very interested in learning more about the client's experience, particularly around fees. He wonders if they can add in two standard questions, "How likely are you to recommend?" and "Why, or why not?" to address the alternative fee structures. Edith explains that the simplicity of the two NPS questions can lead to additional discussions with clients rather than overwhelming them to start.

Chad, the bankruptcy partner, is not keen on the NPS survey at all. He is fine with tracking the bar complaints; in fact, he believes that has been done informally. Edith explains that only Clint and the responsible partner have been made aware of any complaints in the past. She reassured him that in her five years with the firm, there has never been a complaint that has made it past the early first stages.

Chad wonders about potentially pestering the clients to answer long surveys and also thinks clients would respond better to a phone call than an e-mail. Corey, who is the partner in charge of the start-up practice, disagrees, and she is keen on getting the NPS survey launched.

Charles, who oversees the litigation group, is also very interested in obtaining feedback using the NPS. A couple of years ago he started asking clients around 10 questions, like an exit interview approach, and asked them to rate the firm, service level, the fees, and so on using a scale of 1 to 5. Charles explains that the clients were happy to answer the 10 questions. Some of the information was very useful because they found out that the clients were unhappy with the fees. Apparently, there were some surprises in terms of final bills. Ultimately, his team was too busy to follow up with the unanswered questionnaires, and client work took over. However, the group did implement the current fee structure, where they set an upper limit on the case without client approval.

The fifth partner is Candace, who runs the business group, which is about 40% of the firm's revenue. Clint has the largest clients in this group as his practice area is mergers and acquisitions. Candace volunteers her current clients to survey because they have recently implemented new average rates for their clients based on the team servicing the matter. Also, Candace's team has been extremely busy on three large deals, and she is concerned that the other clients may have been ignored.

The firm's client list is within the CRM. The end of engagement letters and the list is divided into prospective clients, current or active clients, and past clients by each of the five partners' practice areas. The clients that may be surveyed total almost 4,000, as there are many small matters in the business and start-up practices.

Edith explains that the NPS is very simple to calculate, and she will use an Excel spreadsheet to enter the numeric responses to calculate the score. NPS survey answers of 1-6 are detractors; 7 or 8 are neutral; and 9 or 10 are promoters. The spreadsheet calculation ignores the neutrals, and it takes the percentage of promoters and subtracts the percentage of detractors to yield a NPS percentage. She believes that some of the issues that Charles' survey encountered should not be repeated because there is just one number to input, and then any answers to the why or why not question will be copied over in a different sheet.

Chad is convinced, and all the partners agree, to support Edith as she rolls out the two questions using Survey Monkey in e-mails and one follow-up call after a week. Clint will write a blog on this new process and commits to sharing the 2016 results. They decide to phase in the survey by quarter for each partner's clients as follows:

Clint—Q3 (Big Business)
Chad—Q4 (Bankruptcy)
Corey—Q2 (Startups)
Charles—Q3 (Litigation)
Candace—Q1 & Q2 (Business)

Candace has also asked to not only survey past clients, but also to survey some of the current clients in order to set a baseline and gather additional data. The partners decide to slowly roll this program out over the year and to include clients from the past 18 months and new clients that have any type of recurring revenue. The rationale is that clients that are on the start-up monthly fee or the flat monthly retainer fee do not really have an end of engagement letter unless they discontinue BUSINESS representation. At that point, they would receive the survey like other clients.

Edith explains that they should only resurvey clients to see any improvement after at least three months if they are on the monthly retainer type of engagement and at the end of the completed additional matter for repeat clients.

Targets

Clint has done some research on the legal field and has heard that the average law firm NPS is well below 50%. He feels that the firm is doing a wonderful job and has a high number of referrals from past clients. Edith makes a note to look into also implementing a client referral rate KPI.

Action: Clint and the partners agree on the target of 70% for the NPS and 50% for the recovery rate. On the bar complaint side, they all agree that the target is naturally zero.

§ 9:6 Firm example: CE BUSINESS—First quarter results

6-CE(a)—Net Promoter Score for the first three months:

CE BUSINESS 2016			
	Jan	Feb	Mar
6-CE(a) Net Promoter Score (%)	18%	24%	50%
TARGET—Net Promoter Score (%)	70%	70%	70%
On scale of 1- 10, how likely to recommend the firm to <others>?			
Input—Total Responses	22	92	68
Input—Promoter (9 or 10)	9	22	42
Input—Neutral (7 or 8)	8	70	18
Input—Detractor (1-6)	5	0	8

Edith sets up a Survey Monkey with both questions and exports an Excel spreadsheet with the numeric and written results. She enlists Candace's paralegal's help, and they send out about 350 surveys over the first three months. Edith uses the CRM's e-mail capabilities to send out the first and then the final request. She spaces the e-mails out by one week, and if there is no answer, she calls only once.

Some of the phone conversations were very informative, but Edith notes that it can take up to 15 minutes to chat with the client. She is careful to ask politely why they did not answer the e-mail request for the survey. Many are not receiving the e-mails, and Edith will check in with the CRM company, as it could be a spam issue.

Overall the results are not at all what was expected. In January there were only 22 responses from almost 80 surveys. The response rate improved to slightly over 50%, and the results climbed from a low of 18% to 50%.

Why or why not responses yielded excellent comments that Edith summarized as follows:

- Prospective clients said that the initial meeting took too long to set up and wondered why the firm did not have an answering service or online calendar tool.
- Monthly retainer clients would like a bit more information on what matters were actually worked on. The bills needed more information.
- Many clients did not like the separate charge for copies and mailings. They understood filing fees but not these internal fees. This comment came from both the hourly clients and the monthly retainer clients.

Edith and Candace met and decide to make the following changes:

Rerun Clint's blog on the website explaining why BUSINESS is contacting its clients for feedback.

Have the survey e-mail come from the appropriate partner or attorney rather than Edith.

Call for response and try to limit the call to a five- or 10-minute maximum. Consider spreading those calls around to the appropriate legal assistant.

6-CE(b)—Client Services Recovery Rate for the first three months is impossible to calculate because the first quarter of 2016 is when the initial 6-CE(a) NPS data is captured and calculated; therefore, there will only be KPI in the second quarter.

CE BUSINESS 2016			
	Apr	May	June
6-CE(b) Client Services Recovery Rate (%)	NA	NA	34%
TARGET—Client Recovery Rate (%)	NA	NA	50%
Repeat Clients NPS Question	NA	NA	NA
Total Detractor & Neutral	13	70	26
Input—From Neutral to Promoter	4	12	13
Input—From Detractor to Promoter	3	5	0

Edith resurveyed Candace's neutrals and detractors after three months. Unfortunately, there was not the improvement that was expected. Candace agreed with Edith's recommendation that the follow-up surveys be done by the legal assistants for neutral and either an associate or partner for the detractors. Anyone who gave the firm a one should receive a call from a partner.

Candace talks to the other partners and recommends that the KPI results be split up by practice areas so each partner can look into their area.

6-CE(c)—Bar Complaints for the first three months:

CE BUSINESS 2016			
	Apr	May	June
6-CE(c) Bar Complaints (#)	0	0	0
TARGET Bar Complaints (#)	0	0	0
Input—# Bar Complaint Received	0	0	0

In the first three months of the year, there have not been any bar complaints. The goal is to resolve any before they move beyond the initial complaint stage.

§ 9:7 Firm example: CE BUSINESS—Full year results

Exhibit 1 at the end of the chapter contains the full year of results. The firm surveyed almost 4,000 clients and received responses from about 60%. The 6-CE(a) NPS was all over the place for the year. However, because the partners had done surveys in various quarters to start, we can see some numbers by partner as outlined below:

	High	Low
Candace:	95%	0%
Corey:	95%	0%
Clint:	81%	23%
Charles:	81%	23%
Chad:	77%	43%

Remember that although Candace volunteered to go first in Q1 and Q2, some of her clients who ended engagements in Q3 and Q4 would be included with the results. The same would be true for Corey in Q3 and Q4 and then Clint and Charles in Q4. Overall the firm was at 46% for the year.

Clint joked that it was a bit of the "careful what you wish for" situation with the responses. Initially everyone was worried that no one would respond, but gathering the numbers and analyzing was just the beginning. About a quarter of the numeric responses were accompanied by a written response to the "why or why not."

When the first year was reviewed, Edith did see a trend towards more online responses and phone calls in the latter half of the year. The follow-up surveys were only by e-mail.

The positive written responses were just as valuable as the why not, or negative-type responses. Starting with the positive, there were simple comments such as: great team; results; affordable; and value for the money. Some negative ones were also very simple: too expensive; bad case outcome; lack of communication; and often not feeling confident in the representation. The latter was a red flag for Edith to dig deeper into who worked on the clients' matter. Other clients wrote a paragraph or two or spent time on the phone with a legal assistant giving detailed positive or negative feedback.

Candace had her legal assistant take the first six months of 6-CE(a) NPS information and break down the numeric NPS results by timekeeper, type of work, and fee structure. Anyone who worked on a client matter would have those NPS results. It was a time-consuming project because so many clients were surveyed. The assistant started with June and worked backwards, noting when the first quarter clients had responded to the second survey for 6-CE(b) Client Services Recovery Rate. Candace met with the attorneys and paralegals to review the analysis in July and then again in December.

By drilling down into the practice area and then into the individual timekeeper, patterns emerged around the feedback. Clients were still confused by the monthly retainer fee structure, and some attorneys were not communicating as much as the clients wished.

It was interesting that Clint's bigger business clients were quick to respond to the survey and were promoters. Those clients could be great ambassadors for the firm. Chad was concerned about the ethics of publishing the results. Candace and Clint assured him that they would be discussing these results on the firm's blog only in aggregate.

Corey's legal assistant borrowed from Candace's analysis for the surveys that were done for her practice. In April, Corey's start-up clients were surveyed, and 85 of the 100 neutral responses were from her clients. They dove into those April comments, which were mainly around fees. The takeaway was that the flat monthly fee should be clearly identified as a subscription model with more details on the website and in their engagement letters. Most of these start-ups are familiar with the subscription model, but the wording used by the law firm was confusing. These start-up clients want after-hours access to the attorneys' calendars.

Finally, the feedback repeatedly asked for electronic billing and document automation. Clint was going to search for existing technology to integrate with his CRM and LPM to address the client concerns. Clint was steadfast in continuing to measure the NPS in 2017 and wanted to keep the 70% target, as in the month of November they had exceeded that target.

Looking at the second KPI 6-CE(b) Client Services Recovery Rate is a good follow-up step for all the partners' practices, but they were reluctant to push the second survey too much. Corey and Candace asked that any second survey for ongoing clients be set for at a minimum of six months after the first result. For the following year, they decided to reduce the goal to one in four, or 25% recovery. The CRM systems allows for the e-mails to be timed, so that automation will be incorporated into 2017.

For KPI 6-CE(c) Bar Complaints there were two complaints within the year. The partners in the other practice areas would never have known about these without the KPI meetings. Both complaints were resolved immediately after being filed. One was as a result of an attorney error, and the second was a misunderstanding with a client billing. Clint decides that they will train the team on these two incidents.

Overall Clint and the partners are pleased with the effort, and Edith is keen to continue, but also delegate some of the survey work to the legal assistants and use as much automation within the LPM and CRM as possible.

Changes:

2017 Process—Rather than surveying all coming from Edith, each partner will run the initial and any follow-up NPS surveys. Edith will aggregate the results and continue to monitor the bar complaints.

Technology Improvements—a small group of attorneys, led by Corey, have created a small group to explore additional technology, particularly to increase transparency in billing through electronic billing, finding onboarding software, client questionnaires, and document automation. Also, Corey will be piloting an online calendar plug-in on the for her start-up clients to book time. The firm will adopt this if the pilot is successful.

Link with Performance and Firm Culture—These KPIs are just the start, and the partners wish to look at the individual performance metrics and firm culture in conjunction with the client experience in 2017.

Training and Mentoring—In addition to technology, the partners realized that they needed to train the attorneys and paralegals on best practices, not just to avoid bar complaints, but to improve communication with clients.

Website—The firm will leverage all the public speaking at events and the firm involvement in the local community by adding in those events to the website and newsletter.

Exhibit 1—Client Experience CE Business

CE BUSINESS 2016	Jan	Feb	Mar	Apr	May	June	July	Aug	Sept	Oct	Nov	Dec	ANNUAL
6-CE(a) Net Promoter Score (%)	18%	24%	50%	0%	37%	95%	81%	23%	60%	45%	77%	43%	46%
TARGET - Net Promoter Score (%)	70%	70%	70%	70%	70%	70%	70%	70%	70%	70%	70%	70%	70%
On scale of 1-10, how likely to recommend the firm to <others>?													
Input - Total Responses	22	92	68	146	386	77	234	377	277	198	225	250	2352
Input - Promoter (9 or 10)	9	22	42	23	170	75	200	104	177	108	198	150	1278
Input - Neutral (7 or 8)	8	70	18	100	187	0	24	254	88	72	2	57	880
Input - Detractor (1 to 6)	5	0	8	23	29	2	10	19	12	18	25	43	194

CE BUSINESS 2016	Jan	Feb	Mar	Apr	May	June	July	Aug	Sept	Oct	Nov	Dec
6-CE(b) Client Services Recovery Rate (%)						34%			23%			35%
TARGET - Client Recovery Rate (%)						50%			50%			50%
Repeat clients NPS question												
Total Detractor & Neutral				13	70	26	123	216	2	34	273	100
Input - From Neutral to Promoter				4	12	13	10	35	15	25	40	60
Input - From Detractor to Promoter				3	5	0	3	7	9	5	3	10

CE BUSINESS 2016	Jan	Feb	Mar	Apr	May	June	July	Aug	Sept	Oct	Nov	Dec	2015
6-CE(c)Bar Complaints (#)	0	0	0	1	0	0	0	0	0	0	1	0	0
TARGET Bar Complaints (#)	0	0	0	0	0	0	0	0	0	0	0	0	0
Input - # Bar Complaint Received	0	0	0	1	0	0	0	0	0	0	1	0	0

§ 9:8 Firm example: CE BUSINESS—Prior year data points

The only data available in the past around NPS was Charles' survey that was very detailed and somewhat incomplete. Edith reviewed the information, but it is not comparable to the NPS calculation. Therefore, the group will go forward only.

In 2015, there were no bar complaints. The partners agree that in 2017 the 6-CE(a) NPS and (b) Client Service Recovery Rate KPIs need to be by practice area, and Edith will work with the legal assistants to break down the 2016 data to create comparable information.

§ 9:9 Technology to assist with client experience KPIs

Properly implemented technology can not only assist with data collection and reduce duplication of tasks, but also improve and streamline law firm workflow or process. Some of the technology that can be used to assist with client experience KPIs includes:

- Excel—to avoid problems with various versions of the same spreadsheet, firms should use a safe shared drive or server and create links between different workbooks and sheets to simplify data input.
- Legal Practice Management (LPM)—the client list information can be generated from the LPM.
- Customer Relationship Management (CRM)—the client list information can be generated from the LPM, and some may allow for surveys to be run from the CRM.
- Online Survey Software—Survey Monkey and Google provide easy and free survey platforms that can export Excel results to integrate with the KPI worksheets or tracking system.
- Calendar—many LPMs and calendars can integrate and synchronize to pass data on follow-up survey timing and related tasks.
- Interview Automation Software—depending on the area of the law, there are various companies which have designed software that collects information from prospective clients on the firm website, thus saving the time.

- Document Automation and Registration—there are various software programs that automate standard document assembly or gather the info for incorporation, family law, or divorce, as examples. When attorneys use these systems, they can automate the tasks that do not require any professional judgment and allow for efficiencies.

A nonexhaustive list of technology resources is in APPENDIX D.

§ 9:10 Common mistakes or pitfalls

The above firm example and other experiences give rise to lessons learned that are set out below as common mistakes or pitfalls to avoid:

- Anonymous surveys. Given the Internet culture of being able to give feedback either through Yelp or other means, people are very used to being surveyed. Without the information on the source, you cannot follow-up to probe deeper or thank your client for feedback. People who take the time to give feedback wish to know that they have been heard.
- Not probing deeper. Some firms only wish to collect the NPS number and do not ask "why or why not." Even though it may create more work, at least you can begin to understand your strengths and weaknesses from independent sources.
- Too much at once. Do not survey all of your clients in the same month. Roll this program out slowly and you can then test what works and what does not work.
- Over-surveying. "Know your audience" always applies. If your clients would be bothered by a second request or a second follow-up survey, then tailor your approach to your clients.
- Under-surveying. If you do survey clients and receive information that is concerning, then perhaps a phone call or other means of follow-up is required rather than just letting their issues be dropped.
- Ignoring trends. A good rule is to not look at the data only one client by one client. Look at all the promoters and what was their why? Do you see some themes? Those good practices should be celebrated and passed on to the team. Similarly look to the neutrals or detractor for themes or consistent issues. I personally have a rule of three; if I hear something from three independent sources, I start paying attention and dig deeper.
- Viewing NPS in isolation. The NPS is an only one metric and should be considered within the entire KPI framework, including individual performance and firm culture.

- Not using the data to promote. Many companies or firms will put their information on their website. For example, NPS scores can be used as a marketing tool in a blog or on the home page.

Our next and final KPI is the measurement of the firm culture. The culture and happiness of your team is directly related to their performance and the delivery of the services to clients.

Chapter 10

Deep Dive KPI 7: Firm Culture (FC)

§ 10:1   Introduction
§ 10:2   KPI 7—Firm culture (FC) summary
§ 10:3   Data and sources
§ 10:4   Background
§ 10:5   Firm example: FC DEFENSE
§ 10:6   —First quarter results
§ 10:7   —Full year results
§ 10:8   —Prior year data points
§ 10:9   Technology to assist with firm culture KPIs
§ 10:10 Common mistakes or pitfalls

§ 10:1   Introduction

Last, but certainly not least, are the KPIs for measuring the health of the firm environment or culture. Much has been written about company culture, and as mentioned previously, your firm is a business. Law is primarily people-based; even with technology, lawyers are still needed.

Ensuring that your team is excited and motivated to come to work every day will impact all the KPIs, particularly the performance and client experience KPIs. Your firm brand and reputation are impacted by your team and aligning your goals and vision within the firm is critical to success.

As an aside, you may think that this chapter will not apply if you are a solo without any support staff. Obviously, you would not be surveying anyone or calculating leverage with other team members. However, you could consider completing an annual self-assessment test and measuring how much you are leveraging technology.

§ 10:2   KPI 7—Firm culture (FC) summary

The seventh and final KPI area on Firm Culture (FC) contains four metrics, as outlined in the table below, and APPENDIX B, Comprehensive KPI Listing—KPI 7: Firm Culture, presents the information in table format with formulas.

§ 10:2   LAW FIRM KEY PERFORMANCE INDICATORS

6-CE Metrics	Calculation	Frequency*
7-FM (a): Average Work Climate Satisfaction (#)	The total of the work climate survey scores divided by the number of surveys	Quarterly
7-FM (b): Employee Involvement (%)	The number of employees participating in company events divided by the total number of employees	Quarterly
7-FM (c): Leverage (%)	Total managing partner billings divided by total firm billings	Quarterly
7-FM (d): Annual Turnover (%)	The number of attorneys and paralegals who left in the year divided by the maximum number of attorneys and paralegals over the year	Annually

* We recommend that KPIs are tracked regularly either monthly, quarterly, or annually once fully implemented. In the early stages of adoption, try to collect as much data as possible monthly and do an assessment at the end of the first quarter, including a comparison to the prior year. Some metrics will lend themselves to monthly measurement, while others will be naturally quarterly or annually. However, each firm's situation will be different, and there is simply no right or wrong approach to measurement; therefore, the frequencies listed in the table are only recommendations or examples.

§ 10:3 Data and sources

The workplace or culture survey will likely be new to the firms. However, with many online tools available, it is not very hard to create something simple to get started using a Survey Monkey or Google Documents survey. Alternatively, there are outside consultants that can be brought in to conduct the surveys for larger firms with more resources.

The rest of the data is relatively simple to collect and does not require any CRM or LPM system. The number of timekeepers and billings will come from the time and billing system or accounting system, and the number of employee event information would be from calendars or kept by the organizer.

§ 10:4 Background

The KPI framework is finishing with internal measures, which have a great impact on clients and your most important component, your team. Regardless of the size of the firm, it is about the legacy that is created by your practice.

People wish to be appreciated and see how they fit into the vision and future of where they work. Law is no different. By committing to review firm culture, you are engaging in succession planning and uncovering the training and human resources needs associated with creating a healthy firm environment.

For Solos:

It seems counterintuitive to measure anything to do with firm culture if you are truly operating alone.

However, I encourage you to do an internal annual inventory as follows:

- What do I love about my practice?
- What do I dread about my practice?
- Where do I see my practice next year? In two years? In five Years?

You can check your answers quarterly or annually and based on the answers, you may find yourself making some changes. Also, I suggest finding a mentor to discuss your vision and answers to the self-assessment above.

Solos are very similar to the entrepreneur because they have to do everything, from the administration, the client development, including sales and marketing, to accounting, planning, and, of course, the practice of law. Therefore, leveraging technology is critical to their survival. Measuring that leverage can be as simple as looking at a solo KPI around performance to see if you can collect more billings without spending more hours working. For example, if you can use technology to create the first draft of a contract or immigration application and you are charging the client based on a flat fee, you will have less time spent on matters for the same money.

However, getting back to the firm environment, the following is an example of how the firm culture KPI can improve your firm success.

§ 10:5 Firm example: FC DEFENSE

Last year two small firms and a solo practitioner merged together to create FC DEFENSE. One of the firms was around

§ 10:5   LAW FIRM KEY PERFORMANCE INDICATORS

for about 15 years before joining with a five-year-old firm and a new solo who only had practiced for 18 months after 10 years in Big Law. The new firm was created in the spring of 2014 and named Fred Cotton as the managing partner. Fred Cotton has 20 years of experience and was from the five-year-old firm. Fred is determined to examine the new firm's culture.

FC DEFENSE are trial attorneys who defend clients for all matters of criminal nature, including driving offenses, which is a significant part of their practice; white collar crime; and all the way up to and including serious felonies, but not capital matters. The firm uses an LPM that includes time and billing. The administrative assistant, Frankie, handles the day-to-day accounting, including billing, but an outside accountant prepares the financial statements and taxes.

Fred has heard some rumblings about the new structure and vision that is effective on January 1st of 2016 and was outlined in a December memo to everyone. Fred wants to invest heavily in local advertising, including television and billboards, to establish the new brand of "First Choice" Defense. He also lets everyone know that he wishes to drastically cut back on the pro bono defense work done by Frank, the former managing partner of the older firm. Faith, the former solo, is vocal about wanting to use social media, particularly Facebook advertising, to reach potential clients. Frank is not opposed, but the majority of his work comes through word of mouth and a referral network.

In the same memo, Fred outlined the partners' expectation as far as individual performance as follows:

Managing Partner—Fred Cotton	75% billable target
Partners—Frank & Faith	75% billable target
Associate Attorneys: Faye, Francine, Felix, Forest, Fitz	90% billable target
Paralegals: Flynn, Fiona, Fox, Frederick, Felicity	90% billable target
Administrative- Frankie	25% billable target

Frankie meets with the three partners to discuss the type of employee survey planned for March 2016. Faith has researched online and found great resources at a site called Tiny Pulse https://www.tinypulse.com/. This company has a listing of 20 questions that employees should be asked. Fred thinks that ques-

tions once a quarter is way too much, and Frank agrees. They discuss and decide upon the following approach:
- Anonymous surveys using Survey Monkey
- A maximum of five questions each quarter with the 1-5 rating scale
- Partners review and respond within one week of the results

Also, the firm has not done any events for just the team; instead they have hosted many client events and expected the FC DEFENSE people to attend. Faye and Felix have indicated an interest in planning these events. The partners agree to a small budget for some employee events but do not want them to impact the client work.

Frank and Faith discuss Fred's billable target percentage that is the same as their targets. Given that the managing partner has additional duties, they believe that this should be a lower target. Fred does not wish to change his billable target, and the partners agree to review the KPI results and discuss it later in the year.

Targets

The partners have no idea what the survey results' target should be. The survey asks for a rating for each question on a scale from 1 to 5, with 5 being the most positive answer. For example, a question similar to the net promoter score (NPS) that is part of the client experience KPI can be tailored as follows:

On a scale of 1 to 5, how likely are you to refer people to work at FC DEFENSE?

Rather than using a calculation like NPS, the answers are totaled and divided by five.

Action: An arbitrary target of 80%, or an average of 4 out of 5, is set. For the employee events, the partners believe that 100% attendance is possible and also say that one person leaving per year, or 10% turnover, is reasonable. Fred's 10% leverage target is set by Frankie's calculation of Fred's billable hours based on the firm-wide 2,000 available hours multiplied by the billable percentage for all timekeepers.

§ 10:6 Firm example: FC DEFENSE—First quarter results

The firm launches the first survey, and the small group plans three events for the team only, one in January and one in March. Two of the attorneys, Francine and Fitz, left the firm in March before the survey, and Fred decided that it was unnecessary for him to complete one. Therefore, 10 surveys were completed.

7-FM(a)—Average Work Climate Satisfaction for the first three months:

FC DEFENSE 2016			
	Jan	Feb	Mar
7-FM(a) Average Work Climate Satisfaction (#)	NA	NA	3.2
TARGET Average Work Climate Satisfaction (#)	NA	NA	4
Rate the firm culture and/or work climate on a scale of 1 to 5 on quarterly basis			
Input—total of all work survey scores			32
Input—number of surveys completed			10

The first survey had asked three questions around how much employees enjoy working at FC DEFENSE, including the "how likely are you to refer" question above plus two around work environment and support. The partners agreed that the survey should be anonymous but did not add in any place for written comments. When the partners drilled into the responses, while the average was 3.2, there was one survey that was all ones as response and another that was an average of two. The partners were at a loss as to what they could do because they did not know the background. It was helpful to know that there are team members that are not happy, but they could not do much other than pose questions. Were people unhappy because of the advertising or marketing strategy, the office situation, or the parking?

Action: Fred agrees that he should do the survey, and the three partners decide to add in the optional "why or why not" so that they can better understand the responses.

Action: Faith asks that Fred and Frank do exit interviews with Francine and Fitz to ask about their reasons for leaving. It has been about a month, but it is a close-knit legal community, and neither associate left on bad terms.

7-FM(b)—**Employee Involvement** for the first three months:

FC DEFENSE 2016			
	Jan	Feb	Mar
7-FM(b) Employee Involvement (%)	NA	NA	88%
TARGET Employee Involvement (%)	NA	NA	100%
Input—Number of Employee Participants	10	0	18
Input—Total Events	1	0	2
Input—Total Number of Employees	12	12	10

The first event was in January around a big case win and was slightly impromptu. Two paralegals could not make it, as they had family commitments. The organizing group set up an event on a Thursday evening and had everyone attend. The second event in late March was a lunch after the two attorneys had left and interfered with client commitments.

Action: Set events with more lead time for planning and do outside of work hours. Faith was going to talk with everyone for suggestions for the events, particularly over the busy summer months.

7-FM(c)—**Leverage** for the first three months:

FC DEFENSE 2016			
	Jan	Feb	Mar
7-FM(c)Leverage (%)	NA	NA	11%
TARGET Leverage (%)	NA	NA	10%
Input—Managing Partner billings			$150,000
Input—Total Billings			$1,397,875

Fred is pleased that he is close to the target, but Frank and Faith explain that they feel that he should be pulling back from billings and focus on growing the firm and creating a succession plan. It is like a CEO of a business: They are externally focused on the vision and the future, not selling and delivering services. They would like to see Fred's target at 6 to 8% and expand the firm billings through new hires. Fred decides to keep the same billable hour target of 75%. The partners agree to discuss at the end of the year and believe that a billable hour target of 50% for

§ 10:6   LAW FIRM KEY PERFORMANCE INDICATORS

Fred and 60% for themselves would free them up to develop the business and the team.

7-FM(d)—Annual Turnover is not calculated until there is a full year of results, although the partners were disappointed with the two departures in March.

§ 10:7 Firm example: FC DEFENSE—Full year results

Exhibit 1 at the end of the chapter contains the details of the full year, and the summary for 7-FC(a) is below. The questions were varied and spaced out over each quarter, so each one had a theme:

- Q1: Enjoyment—Three questions
- Q2: Career Path—Four questions
- Q3: Team—Three questions
- Q4: Feedback & Enjoyment—Three questions

FC DEFENSE 2016	Q1	Q2	Q3	Q4
Average Work Climate Satisfaction (#)—Q	3.2	3.0	4.2	3.9
TARGET Average Work Climate Satisfaction (#)	4	4	4	4

It appears from the survey results above that the employee involvement and the annual turnover are all linked. Over the year there were three departures, two attorneys in the first quarter, and then Felicity, a late 2015 paralegal hire, left in November.

At a very high level, although the survey results overall were close to the target, there seems to be some issues with career path. The surveys were done anonymously because the partners wanted honest feedback. The first quarter there was no place for people to comment on the survey. The partners decided to put in a "why or why not" with each of the questions starting in the second quarter. The second survey was done in June, and the results were even lower than Q1.

In fact, some of the Q2 survey comments were directed at uncertainty about the future growth of FC DEFENSE because Fred wishes to remain 75% billable along with the other two partners.

When the firm meets in early July, the partners end up apologizing for not following up with some actions from the Q1 survey. They did release the numeric results but then were tied

Deep Dive KPI 7: Firm Culture (FC) § 10:7

up hiring to replace the two associates. Faith has researched that doing nothing after a survey is worse than not doing the survey at all.

In the meeting, there is talk about the Q2 survey results, and the more senior associates are concerned that they are not being groomed for partnership. The paralegals continue to be concerned that they are not able to bill as much as expected because enough work is not delegated. The survey has prompted dialogue, and the partners commit to an action plan around career development for late July.

The Q3 team questions yield the highest results yet for the survey. Several respondents indicate that they are pleased with the new hires and the efforts being made around mentoring and training. One person does appreciate that no employee events were scheduled in July and August because the firm is so short staffed.

In the final quarter, the survey repeats the same "how likely are you to refer" question above plus a couple around performance feedback and the usefulness of the survey itself. This time the "why or why not" was included, but the survey remained anonymous. There was no score below a three, in comparison to the one and twos from the first quarter. However, there was much feedback about Fred's television campaigns; it was the general consensus that Faith's more modern social media advertising and marketing strategy should be pursued.

The partners debate whether they can move from an anonymous survey. Faith is all for moving to one-to-one meetings, but Frank thinks it is too soon and may never be the best approach. Clint casts the deciding vote to keep things anonymous. They are pleased with the new attorney hires and feel that the survey is helping them better understand the needs of the team.

The employee involvement has improved over the year, and the partners were very pleased that the September event had 100% attendance. There were almost the same results in October and December, but illness took out a few team members.

The exit interviews with the attorneys had yielded some good feedback around a lack of career path and mentoring. When the paralegal Felicity had her exit interview in November, she cited the lack of work and life balance as the main factor for leaving. In addition, she was very busy but still struggled to hit her billable target. The work was not being delegated from the attorneys properly.

The partners discuss the leverage issues again given the information from Felicity and some of the comments from the survey.

Fred agrees to reduce his billable hours and focus on growing the team and delegating additional work. Both Faith and Frank will also reduce their hours and only try to seek out the work that only they can complete.

Frankie shares some of the other new KPI data that was gathered for client experience and noted that there was a correlation between 7-FC(a) and the net promoter score (NPS). Over the year there was an increase in both.

Changes:

Formalize Succession Planning. The partners agree to set up a plan for their eventual retirement even though for Faith that might be 20 years away.

Mentoring, Professional Development, and Training Plans. Each partner is now responsible for mentoring an associate and paralegal. Faith encourages the partners to set regular meetings and provide guidance on professional development, career path advice, and training needs. If in these one-to-one meetings some of the culture issues are brought up, they can be brought to the partners anonymously.

Exit Interviews. Every person will have an exit interview within a week of giving notice.

Streamline Survey. Do quarterly surveys, but have the questions modified so that each question is asked twice per year in a rotating fashion. Continue asking why or why not questions.

Deep Dive KPI 7: Firm Culture (FC) § 10:7

Exhibit 1—Firm Culture

FIRM CULTURE

FC DEFENSE 2016

	Jan	Feb	Mar	Apr	May	June	July	Aug	Sept	Oct	Nov	Dec
7-FC(a) Average Work Climate Satisfaction (#)			3.2			3.0			4.2			3.9
TARGET Average Work Climate Satisfaction (#)			4			4			4			4
Rate the firm culture and/or work climate on a scale of 1 to 5 on												
Input - total of all work survey scores			32			36			50			47
Input - number of surveys completed			10			12			12			12

FC DEFENSE 2016

	Jan	Feb	Mar	Apr	May	June	July	Aug	Sept	Oct	Nov	Dec
7-FC(b) Employee Involvement (%)			88%			95%			100%			94%
TARGET Employee Involvement (%)			100%			100%			100%			100%
Input - number of employee participants	10	0	18	9	11	0	0	0	12	23	0	11
Input - total events	1	0	2	1	1	0	0	0	1	2	0	1
Input - total number of employees	12	12	10	10	11	12	12	12	12	12	11	12

FC DEFENSE 2016

	Jan	Feb	Mar	Apr	May	June	July	Aug	Sept	Oct	Nov	Dec
7-FC(c) Leverage (%)			11%			13%			13%			11%
TARGET Leverage (%)			10%			10%			10%			10%
Input - Managing Partner billings			$150,000			$155,000			$145,000			$150,000
Input - Total billings			$1,397,875			$1,220,675			$1,097,500			$1,405,600

FC DEFENSE 2016

	Jan	Feb	Mar	Apr	May	June	Jul	Aug	Sept	Oct	Nov	Dec
7-FC(d) Annual Turnover (%)												27%
TARGET - Annual Turnover (%)												10%
Input - number of associates and paralegals who left during the year												3
Maximum number of associates and paralegals over the year												11

§ 10:8 Firm example: FC DEFENSE—Prior year data points

There are only data points for 7-FC(c) Leverage and 7-FC(d) Annual Turnover from prior years.

Frankie pulls together the annual results for 2014 and 2015, which are 20% and 23%, respectively. When compared to the 2016 results that average about 12%, there has been significant improvement in this area. This improvement makes sense, as in 2014 there were fewer attorneys and paralegals than in 2016, but in 2015, one of the paralegals was on leave for nine months and one attorney left and was not replaced for six months.

Turnover continues to be about 20 per year over those two years. The partners hope with the new work climate survey and timely follow-up actions that the turnover will be reduced in 2017.

§ 10:9 Technology to assist with firm culture KPIs

Properly implemented technology can not only assist with data collection and reduce duplication of tasks, but also improve and streamline law firm workflow or process. Some of the technology that can be used to assist with firm culture KPIs includes:

- Excel—to avoid problems with various versions of the same spreadsheet, use a safe shared drive or server, and create links between different workbooks and sheets to simplify data input.
- Online Survey Software—Survey Monkey and Google provide easy and free survey platforms that can export Excel results to integrate with the KPI worksheets or trackingsystem.

A nonexhaustive list of technology resources is in APPENDIX D.

§ 10:10 Common mistakes or pitfalls

The above firm example and other experiences give rise to lessons learned that are set out below as common mistakes or pitfalls to avoid:

- Too much too soon. Overloading your employees and fellow attorneys with too many surveys that are too detailed. The idea is to get started but only when you have the resourcesto properly follow-up.

- **Lack of follow-up.** There is much research that shows that the backlash from surveying employees without anyfollow-up or feedback is worse than just not doing the survey.
- **Viewing issues in isolation.** Culture and environment impacts everything from individual performance to client experience. Check the overall picture before taking action.
- **Lack of firm training and support.** If your firm is large enough to hire resources to help build a good culture, this can be a wise investment. If not, reading business books and blogs on the subject will help immensely.
- **Absence of career path or mentoring.** Most people leave their positions because of the culture or recognition, not money.

That is the last of the seven KPIs in the framework. Next is a review of the art of setting targets, followed by an implementation plan.

Chapter 11

Setting Targets

§ 11:1 Introduction

An old adage from law school applies here. When I am asked what should the target be, the answer is, "It depends." What is your goal as a lawyer? Is it to practice 3,000 hours a year and retire early? To go for it with contingency fees only? Or to work 40 or fewer hours and spend time outside of the office with family and friends? What lifestyle do you want? Decide your own vision if you are a solo. Within a firm, there needs to be discussion and consensus on each partner's lifestyle goals.

The second adage is to just get started. This is not rocket science; it is not even accounting! You will need to start somewhere, and looking at historical data is a great place. Go back and analyze the most recent full year with readily available data. Or, if you do not have a prior period, run the numbers for the first three months in the current year.

Next, set initial targets based on what you wish to achieve and believe is achievable. Goal setting, again, is linked to the lifestyle and firm culture. However, do not ignore the interdependence of the targets. If your focus is on spending more time on client acquisition, you need to look at your performance KPIs to make sure that the available hour targets set there allow for that extra time on client development.

Revisit the targets each month for the first year and then make the KPIs part of your budgeting process.

Finally, these are your targets and they are never set in stone. If you are a solo, you can adjust them as you go. However, if you are working with a team, it is critical to not only get initial buy-in on targets, but also to review any changes with everyone involved. Below is a set of sample targets made up for a small firm.

If you are a solo, then you can just ignore the KPIs that are not relevant to having one attorney as the only member of the firm.

Exhibit 1—Sample KPI Targets

Key Performance Indicators (KPIs)	Target
1—CLIENT DEVELOPMENT	
1-CD (a): New Client Conversion Rate	≥ 50%
1-CD (b): Client Referral Rate (%)	≥ 25%
1-CD (c): Prospect Client Pipeline (#)	≥ 10
1-CD (d): Adjusted Prospect Pipeline ($)	≥ $500,000
2—CLIENT ACQUISITION COSTS	
2-CAC (a): Client Acquisition Cost (CAC) ($)	≤ $500
2-CAC (b): Upsell Rate (%)	≥ 20%
2-CAC (c): Client Lifetime or Annual Value (CLV) ($)	≥ $50,000
2-CAC (d): CLV to CAC Ratio (#)	≥ 10
3- PRODUCTIVITY	
3-PROD (a): Client Pipeline (#)	≥ 15
3-PROD (b): Revenue per Matter ($)	≥ $7,500
3-PROD (c): Rent Expense (%)	≤ 5%
3-PROD (d): Attorney Leverage (%)	≥ 45%
3-PROD (e): Paralegal Leverage (%)	≥ 55%
3-PROD (f): Attorneys' Productivity (%)	≥ 90%
3-PROD (g): Paralegals' Productivity (%)	≥ 95%
4- PROFITABILITY	
4-PROF (a): Return on Owner Equity (Investment) (ROI) (%)	≥ 25%
4-PROF (b): Contribution Margin ($)	≥ $2,500
4-PROF (c): Profitability Margin (%)	≥ 20%
4-PROF (d): Payroll Ratio (%)	≤ 40%
4-PROF (e): Overhead Ratio (%)	≤ 10%
4-PROF (f): Aging Tolerance (%)	≥ 5%
4-PROF (g): Work in Progress (WIP) Lockup Days (#)	≤ 30
4-PROF (h): Accounts Receivable (A/R) Lockup Days (#)	≤ 30
4-PROF (i): Year over Year Revenue Growth (%)	≥ 10%
4-PROF (j): Revenue per Employee ($)	≥ $250,000
4-PROF (k): Revenue per Attorney ($)	≥ $450,000

Key Performance Indicators (KPIs)	Target
5- PERFORMANCE	
5-PERF (a): Billings Collected by Attorney (%)	≥ 99%
5-PERF (b): Billings Collected by Paralegal (%)	≥ 99%
5-PERF (c): Net Collection by Attorney ($/Hour)	≥ $250
5-PERF (d): Net Collection by Paralegal ($/Hour)	≥ $125
5-PERF (e): Hourly Billings by Attorney ($/Hour)	≥ $250
5-PERF (f): Hourly Billings by Paralegal ($/Hour)	≥ $125
5-PERF (g): Hourly Revenue Collected by Attorney ($/Hour)	≥ $250
5-PERF (h): Hourly Revenue Collected by Paralegal ($/Hour)	≥ $150
6- CLIENT EXPERIENCE	
6-CE (a): Net Promoter Score (NPS) (%)	≥ 60%
6-CE (b): Client Services Recovery Rate (%)	≥ 25%
6-CE (c): Bar Complaints (#)	0
7- FIRM CULTURE	
7-FM (a): Average Work Climate Satisfaction (#)	≥ 4
7-FM (b): Employee Involvement (%)	≥ 90%
7-FM (c): Leverage (%)	≤ 20%
7-FM (d): Annual Turnover (%)	≤ 0%

Chapter 12

Implementation and Continuous Improvement

§ 12:1 Introduction
§ 12:2 Getting started
§ 12:3 Measurement of return on investment (ROI) from tech and KPIs investment
§ 12:4 Continuous KPI measurement
§ 12:5 Be Prepared for Change

§ 12:1 Introduction

In the perfect world, there would be an application or dashboard that you could log into each day with your entire client workflow on display. Magically, all of the KPIs, or the majority of those included in the framework above, would be at your fingertips at either an individual timekeeper, department, or firm level.

However, that would still not get around the fact that KPI implementation leads to change. Sometimes there are surprises, and other times hunches are confirmed with the KPI results. Having the right data and calculations is only useful if you are open to exploring the results and making changes. There are many examples of changes in the seven firms included in the deep dive chapters.

At larger law firms, there are software products that can pull all the data from your various systems to display in one place but unfortunately those products are expensive. Also, many solos and small firms do not have a legal practice management system (LPM) to link to dashboard software. Although it is still possible to measure all of the KPIs in this framework, even without a LPM, I recommend investigating a simple cloud based system. This applies even if you are a solo, and some would argue that it is even more important, because it will free you up from administration to practice law.

Follow the standard management model of "Plan, Do, Check, Act" but call it "Budget, Practice, Measure, Act" and repeat. Review your KPIs as measured on a monthly basis, paying particular attention to what is driving the results. That will lead to continuous improvement.

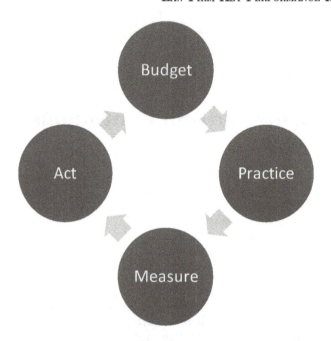

§ 12:2 Getting started

In my life and businesses, we have a motto that says JFDI (just freaking do it). It applies to KPIs. Do not wait until you have the perfect system or all the data, just get started and start small. I recommend doing a least two KPIs from each of the seven areas. Although this book describes seven different firm scenarios, the KPIs are interdependent, and the results should be reviewed in aggregate before taking any action. Otherwise you run the risk of fixing one area at the expense of another.

A KPI framework, whether done on a piece of paper, in a spreadsheet, or with an integrated dashboard, will lead to change, and like all processes, a plan, so start with an Excel workbook. The full KPIs and formulas are listed in APPENDIX B. You can even make your own dashboards in Excel.

I recommend that you start with the measurements in each category and only do those for a year. If the full list in APPENDIX B is too much for you, you could reduce in productivity and profitability areas. Remember some of the data is collected for the entire year, so it may be a while before you have any results. That is why it is a good idea to go back a year to have some baseline information. While keeping the measurement simple facilitates corrective actions, if you only measure one KPI per area, you may not be able to interpret the results.

Displaying data in simple graphs makes it easy for timekeepers to monitor progress. For example, Allan's and Larry's results from the PERFORM REAL ESTATE example outlined in Chapter 8.4 are in graph form using Excel. The full year results from Chapter 8.6 are displayed with the targets in solid lines and the actuals are dashed lines on the following page. Both Allan and Larry can monitor their individual progress visually and ask for more information if needed.

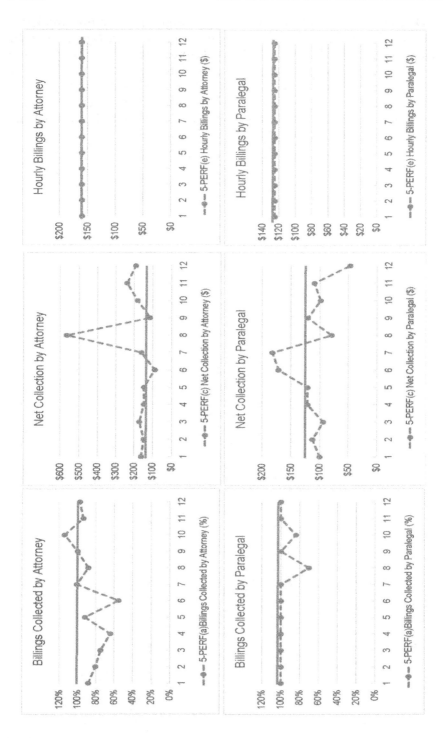

The graphs on the following page are generated in Excel from the KPI data in previous chapters with the gray lines being targets and the black lines are the actual results:

    6-CE(a): Net Promoter Score—Chapter 9.6
    1-CD(b): Client Referral Rate—Conversion Rate—Chapter 4.6
    7-FM(a): Work Climate Satisfaction—Chapter 10.6
    2-CAC(a): Client Acquisition Cost—Chapter 5.10
    6-PROD (a): Client Pipeline—Chapter 6.6
    6-PROD (b): Revenue per Matter—Chapter 6.6

§ 12:2   Law Firm Key Performance Indicators

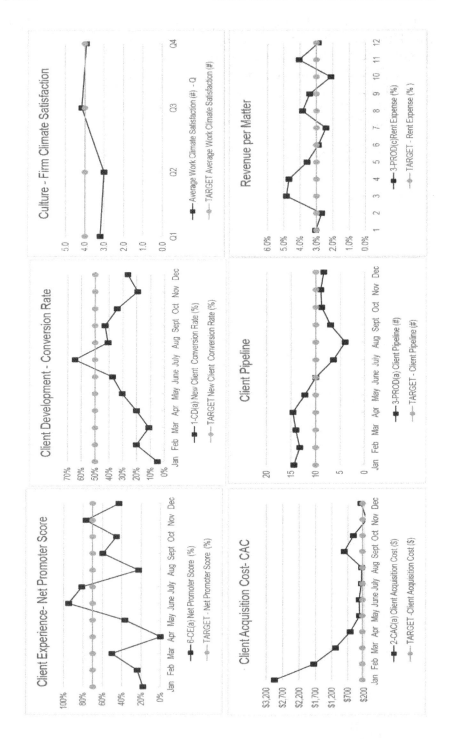

IMPLEMENTATION AND CONTINUOUS IMPROVEMENT   § 12:4

Also, there may be a tendency to take each measure and expand upon it. For example, with respect to the 2-CAC (b): Upsell Rate, it might interest you to know the total dollar value of the new business from those clients. Then, in turn, then you may wish to compare that dollar value to the average client lifetime value.

§ 12:3 Measurement of return on investment (ROI) from tech and KPIs investment

Lawyers are hesitant to implement technology because of a misconception that technology will replace attorneys. In 2012, the American Bar Association adopted a change to the Model Rules of Professional Conduct that imposes a duty of technological competence on attorneys, and this has been adopted in 21 states as of June 2016. The duty includes understanding the risks and benefits and does not force attorneys to use technology in their practices.

Most legal technology providers are working to improve efficiency or generate more business for attorneys, which in turn provides a better client experience without eliminating the lawyer. Back-end technology is critical for a solo—leveraging automation can be a huge win for freeing up the attorney to practice law. In APPENDIX D, there are some technology providers listed that can help with efficient delivery of the law.

I am a proponent of using technology to improve the client experience and the bottom line, but if you cannot measure the ROI, how do you know what is working for your practice? It comes back to the business of legal. Purchasing technology should be measured as any other investment, and firms must have a good system to measure the efficiency and other impacts of the technology. KPIs can assist in identifying areas where technology can support the practice.

§ 12:4 Continuous KPI measurement

The ultimate goal is not just to measure the KPIs, but to make changes to the business processes associated with your law practice to improve results. By measuring what is important to your practice, any changes are data-driven. However, do not act too quickly unless your firm is in financial trouble. Using last year's results in addition to the current year will give you a baseline, but look for trends unless there are obvious outlier results, like the partners' contribution margin difference in PROF PI in Chapter 7.6 or Charlie's high cost of contribution margin inCAC IP in Chapter 5.10.

It sounds counterintuitive, but do not be too quick to change processes radically. Wholesale changes should be based on a trend. For example, if you wish to stop providing a free consultation used to attract clients, gather the appropriate data from your KPIs first. Make small tweaks to your processes and remeasure.

Consider borrowing from the software world's A/B testing model. You can try out experiments on different types of clients based on their profiles and use of technology. Perhaps those that come in from the website would be more suited to use technology to self-assess their legal needs than those who called in or stopped by your practice.

Transparency with your team or involving your accountant can be very helpful. Often those working closest with the clients can identify better processes and systems to help improve your practice. Like any other change process, KPI implementation is not a linear process. It may feel a bit more like pulling on a loose piece of yarn in a sweater: Things may start to unravel before they are all put back together.

§ 12:5 Be Prepared for Change

Why would you implement all these measures if you did not wish to make your practice better? The first implementation of new measurements is like being at the beach and skipping a rock across the surface. It jumps very quickly, and in the same way, you should view the KPIs on the surface in aggregate first. You can then dig deeper and tailor the framework for your firm's immediate pain points. In APPENDIX C there is an outline of a workshop approach to implementation.

The final word is to adopt the KISS (Keep it Super Simple) principle and get started!

Chapter 13

Going International

§ 13:1 International applications

The KPI framework was originally designed for a US-based law solo or small law firm based on years of experience and research in and outside the legal profession. As I recently discussed the framework and approach with international attorneys and experts, it became apparent that the concepts and calculations for these KPIs, for the most part, are transferable to almost any other country, with some tweaks to the terminology.

In the glossary in APPENDIX A, the terms used in this book are defined, and I have attempted to explain some of the American terms, such as retainer, revenue, accounts receivable, owners' or partner accounts, and flat fees, with reference to other known similar terms.

In the United States, the firms are not allowed to take outside investment from nonlawyers, and the firms are set up as partnerships, giving rise to owners, partners, or shareholders. That concept does not impact the KPI methodology or calculations other than perhaps 4-PROF(a) Return on Owner Equity (Investment), which needs to be adjusted to be a traditional return on investment calculation.

As outlined above, the U.S. has several accounting methods, and that will impact the numbers used for revenue, depending on how the revenue is recognized. To my knowledge, other countries do not use the cash method. However, regardless of revenue recognition method, the productivity, profitability, and performance KPIs are designed to focus on cash collections, which is universal.

Appendixes

Appendix A.	Glossary | Translator of Acronyms & Terms
Appendix B.	Comprehensive KPI Listing—KPI 1: Client Development
Appendix C.	Comprehensive KPI Listing—KPI 2: Client Acquisition Costs
Appendix D.	Comprehensive KPI Listing—KPI 3: Productivity
Appendix E.	Comprehensive KPI Listing—KPI 4: Profitability
Appendix F.	Comprehensive KPI Listing—KPI 5: Performance
Appendix G.	Comprehensive KPI Listing—KPI 6: Client Experience
Appendix H.	Comprehensive KPI Listing—KPI 7: Firm Culture
Appendix I.	Implementation Workshop Outline
Appendix J.	Technology Resources
Appendix K.	Intersection with Firm Central & KPI Implementation Plan
Appendix L.	Small Law Firm KPI/Benchmarking Practices Survey Questions (June 2016)
Appendix M.	Resources

APPENDIX A

Glossary | Translator of Acronyms & Terms

United States

Alternative Fee Arrangement (AFA) Fees that are billed on a basis other than time and billing rates without an upper limit. Examples are contingent fees; fixed or flat fees based on representation or work product creation; fixed costs pricing; project rate fees; and monthly or annual subscription fees for defined services.

Accounts Payable (A/P) Amount owing to your vendors for your purchases during the month that are unpaid at the end of the month. Appears as a liability on the balance sheet.

Accounts Receivable (A/R) Amount billed to your clients and owing to you at the end of the month if the bill remains unpaid. Appears as an asset on the balance sheet. In countries other than the U.S., this can be termed "Debtors."

Accrual Basis The accounting method that is the opposite of the cash basis. Under the accrual method, when you commit to an expense you record it as a liability regardless of when you disburse the cash. On the revenue side, in simplified terms, all the revenue that can be realized from the time recorded would be recognized, regardless of what is actually billed and when the cash is received. If you billed $100,000 of time in one year but do not get paid until the following year, you would still pay taxes even though the cash is received in that following year. Most small firms in the U.S. do not use full accrual basis but use a modified accrual basis or the cash basis, and this is unique to the U.S. Taxes are beyond the scope of this book.

Assets The bank accounts, investments, client trust account, equipment, leasehold improvements, computers, cars, etc., on a balance sheet—any item owned by the firm is listed at its historical value less any depreciation or amortization.

Balance Sheet (B/S) The balance sheet is a listing of all the assets and liabilities plus the equity in the firm as at the end of a period, either month's end or firm year's end. The balance sheet is usually produced monthly and accompanied by an income state-

185

ment as well as sometimes a statement of cash inflows and outflows.

Billings | Billed Time Time is recorded and billed. The fees are earned by performing work, and the related time is billed, or the bill for the associated project or flat fees is created and sent to the client. Once the time is billed or billing created, the time is no longer in Work in Progress (WIP) or considered unbilled time; it becomes Accounts Receivable (A/R).

Cash Basis The accounting method where expenses and revenues are only recorded when the check is cut or the cash is received. This basis is the opposite of accrual basis. For law firms, it means if you bill out $100,000 in one year but do not get paid until the following year, you would not recognize the revenue until the cash is received in that following year. For tax purposes, that means that you would not have to pay taxes until the cash is received. Taxes are beyond the scope of this book.

Case | Matter | Project Each client may have more than one project, case, or matter. It is usually the smallest unit of work for a client, and there is normally an engagement letter and billing associated with each matter.

Client = Customer Client and customer are synonymous terms, and while an attempt was made to use "client" consistently, when the term "customer" is used, it means client.

Client Acquisition Cost (CAC) The cost of acquiring a client is calculated by including the sales and marketing costs, plus the billable value of any free attorney or paralegal time, plus direct administrative billable value. CAC is then compared to the potential Client Value as either annual or lifetime potential billings.

Client Value or Lifetime Client Value (CLV) The estimated value of a client for the entire duration of the relationship over multiple matters. In some areas of the law, it is only one matter and then you would be done with the client, so it is necessary to estimate the average matter revenue. In other practices, a client can have multiple matters and you can estimate the overall revenue. When first starting a practice or implementing KPIs, you can use the annual client value to estimate life-time value for multiple-matter clients and refine as you go along. CLV is compared to the Client Acquisition Cost to evaluate client development process.

Costs Agreement is a term used in Australia and New Zealand for the financial arrangement. See the Retainer definition below.

Direct Costs The accounting term used to classify costs related to the delivery of a product or service. For a law firm, the payroll cost for those lawyers and staff for time spent representing a client on a matter would be considered direct costs. Direct costs are included in a calculation of gross margin, but indirect costs are not included.

Draws Often owners or partners in a law firm take draws throughout the year from the partnership. Those draws differ from regular payroll salaries for employees.

Employee An employee is different from a consultant or an owner/partner; an employee is hired and paid on salary with appropriate taxes and employee benefits.

Expenses Almost all outflows from the firm, whether for direct or indirect firm costs, are expenses, with the exception of capital purchases or repayments of debt. Capital purchases are fixed assets like buildings, furniture, and equipment, and the total outlay for those outflows are not recorded as expenses. Instead a portion or an annual depreciation or amortization, based on an estimated life for the asset, is recorded as an expense each year.

Fixed Expenses (or Fixed Costs) A committed cost that must be paid each month based on a contract or other commitment. Malpractice insurance is a fixed cost.

Flat Fees A set amount for a specific representation, service, or work product that is not directly tied to billable hours. For example, the law firm will represent a client for $5,000 for a child custody case. Please note that certain ethical rules may have an impact on flat fees, but that is beyond the scope of this book.

Gross Margin (GM) Product or service revenue less direct costs gives the gross margin on either a business, product, service, and so on. Gross margin is often shown as both a dollar value and a percentage. For law, all legal revenue less direct-matter costs would yield a gross margin for the firm, and that can also be calculated by practice group, lawyer, client, and even matter.

Hard Costs (vs. Soft Costs) These terms are sometimes used synonymously with direct and indirect costs. A hard cost is the same as a direct cost and attributable to a client or delivery of a product. A soft cost is then like indirect costs, and it is not directly related to a client, more like overhead, such as accounting fees.

Income Statement (I/S) An income statement lists all the revenue and expenses for a period of time, either a month or year to date. Revenue and expenses can be included on a cash, accrual, or modified accrual basis. The income statement is usually produced monthly and accompanied by a balance sheet and sometimes a statement of cash inflows and outflows.

Indirect Costs The accounting term used to classify costs that are not attributable to one client or matter but rather supportive of the firm or practice group. Accounting fees or space rental are examples of indirect costs. Indirect costs are often considered overhead costs and are not included in the gross margin calculations.

Interest on Lawyers Trust Accounts (IOLTA) Accounts that are marked as trust are holding client funds and are subject to state bar rules. Anything to do with trust accounts must be accounted for and reconciled regularly.

Key Performance Indicators (KPIs) Different from financial statements, KPIs are metrics used to manage a business. KPIs should represent the entire client lifecycle to include business development, delivery of product or service, company and individual performance, and client satisfaction or experience, as well as profitability.

KPI 1—Client Development metrics measure the efficiency of developing new business, including the creation of a client pipeline.

KPI 2—Client Acquisition Costs metrics not only measure the cost of acquiring new business but also the amount of additional business from existing clients and the overall client value.

KPI 3—Productivity looks at whether the timekeepers have a sufficient backlog of work and whether time and facilities are being used efficiently.

KPI 4—Profitability measures return for the owners and partners and the costs of the business using business concepts such as ratios, aging, and lockup days.

KPI 5—Performance metrics are individual efforts and focus on realization and cash collection rather than utilization.

KPI 6—Client Experience metrics are borrowed from consumer products and software and use the net promoter score (NPS) and follow-up surveys plus bar complaints.

KPI 7—Firm Culture measures rely on surveys, leverage, and turnover metrics to evaluate the workplace.

KISS principle—Keep It Super Simple The overarching principle of this book is KISS, which is to start small and at a high level and only dig into the details where issues are spotted.

Leverage In the law, this means that partners hire associates, paralegals, and assistants to fulfill the client work at a less expensive spend. By leveraging less expensive resources and minimizing expenses, profits can be maximized, but it can also free the partners up to grow their practice. Technology can also be used as leverage in the practice of law.

Liabilities The amounts owing to vendors, tax agencies, banks, and clients for trust account that are listed on the balance sheet as the amount owing as of the end of the period.

Lockup Days is a term used to describe the days when your billable time is locked up in either Unbilled Time (also known as WIP) or Accounts Receivable before it is either billed or collected.

Matter | Case | Project Each client may have more than one project, case, or matter. It is usually the smallest unit of work for a client, and there is normally an engagement letter and billing associated with each matter.

Modified Accrual Basis The accounting method that falls somewhere between the cash basis and accrual basis. There are no official Modified Accrual Basis rules, like the Generally Accepted Accounting Principles (GAAP), that cover the accrual basis, and, therefore, firms can set their own internal policies. Generally, it means that firms recognize revenue when the bills are sent out as Accounts Receivable and recognize expenses as Accounts Payable when the commitment is made, like the regular accrual basis. Firms are not recognizing Work in Progress (WIP) or unbilled time as revenue.

Net Promoter Score (NPS) A concept developed outside of the legal space, often for consumer goods and services, and based on the notion that the best predictor of client satisfaction is how likely they are to recommend you to friends, family, or colleagues.

Nonbillable Time Hours that are spent on activities that are not to be billed to clients. For example, some firms track administrative time spent in meetings or client-development time when free consultations are given to potential clients.

Opportunity Cost In this context, when valuing a free consultation, the billing rate or revenue foregone should be the amount shown as the cost of the free consultation. In other words, if a lawyer gives away a 30-minute consultation and normally bills $200 per hour, the cost of that consultation is the $100 which could have been earned if he or she were billing someone else during that time period. The cost is not the lawyer's salary for the 30 minutes, but the revenue or opportunity lost by giving away the potentially billable time.

Overhead The accounting term for costs that are part of running the overall business or firm, as opposed to the costs of delivering the product or services to the clients. Also can be considered the indirect, or soft, costs. Rent, insurance, communications, marketing, and so on are considered overhead. Like indirect costs, overhead is not used when calculating gross margin.

Owners' Accounts Owners can be partners or shareholders depending on the legal entities, and likely have put money into the firm. Each owner has an account that tracks contributions, draws, and other payments over time.

Partner Accounts Owners can be partners or shareholders depending on the legal entities, and likely have put money into the firm. Each partner has an account that tracks contributions, draws, and other payments over time.

Payments (Over | Under) When payments are made by clients, under the cash basis the revenue is recognized, but under the accrual method, the revenue was recognized when the bill was sent out. If the client under or over pays, there has to be a review to see if the revenue needs to be adjusted.

Payroll The process of paying employees using a system that automatically transfers the money and remits the taxes to the appropriate agencies. Payroll systems are often separate from accounting but should be integrated for ease of compliance and reporting.

Pipeline A listing of all the potential clients that are actively being pursued with an estimated value of the work is used to evaluate client development activities.

Project | Matter | Case Each client may have more than one project, case, or matter. It is usually the smallest unit of work for a client, and there is normally an engagement letter and billing associated with each matter.

Referral Either existing or former clients, other attorneys, or vendors send potential clients as referrals. Some referrals are from paid sources, and the source of all new clients, including referrals, should be tracked by type.

Retainer (Including Evergreen Retainer) Retainers and evergreen (automatically replenishing) retainer are payments made as deposits or down payments by clients. These deposits are not immediately considered revenue. Retainers are different from having a lawyer "on retainer." The latter is when you pay a firm an annual or monthly amount to handle routine legal questions and matters. Overseas a retainer is similar to the Costs Agreement.

Return on Investment (ROI) If you invest $100 and receive $10 back at the end of a year, the ROI is 10% ($10/$100).

Revenue The fees charged for your firm's services. The timing of the revenue recognition is either cash (when the money is received), accrual (when the work is completed), or modified accrual (when the work is complete and billed) in the United States. Revenue is the same as "turnover," a term that may be used in some countries, but here "turnover" is used for staff departures.

Salary Amounts paid to employees as opposed to vendors, such as consultants or contractors.

Soft Costs (vs. Hard Costs) These terms are sometimes used synonymously with direct and indirect costs. A soft cost is similar to an indirect cost, and it is not directly related to a client, more like overhead, such as the accounting fee. A hard cost is then the same as a direct cost and attributable to a client or delivery of a product.

Subscription Fees Ongoing fees for a service or product that are either billed to a client or paid by the firm for services. Therefore, subscription fees can be revenue, as alternative fee arrangements, or expenses, as costs paid to vendors.

Trust Account Accounts that are marked as trust are holding client funds and are subject to state bar rules. Anything to do with trust accounts must be accounted for and reconciled regularly.

Turnover A term to describe personnel turnover and WIP or A/R turnover. Personnel turnover is when attorneys or staff leave the firm. WIP or A/R Turnover is the transfer of WIP to billings or A/R to cash, respectively. In this book, the term "turnover" is not used to mean revenue.

Unbilled Time | Work in Progress (WIP) As timekeepers record their time, it builds up as unbilled or as a work in progress by client. When billing occurs, even if flat fee, that time is moved from unbilled or WIP to accounts receivable. It is good practice to regularly review WIP to ensure that all the time can be billed; otherwise it should be written off.

Vendor | Outside Contractor | Law Firm as a Vendor Vendors and outside contractors are not employees. The law firm itself is a vendor for purposes of the clients. Payments to vendors and outside contractors, including consultants, are not subject to payroll taxes and filings. Classification of workers as contractors versus employees is complex and outside of the scope of this book.

Variable Expenses or Costs A cost that is discretionary and not committed. The cost can vary based on a decision or level of activity. If a firm decides to advertise on the radio for one week, that decision led to the expense and is a variable cost. The cost varies with the decision. This is the opposite of a fixed, or committed, cost.

APPENDIX B

Comprehensive KPI Listing—KPI 1: Client Development

App. B

Key Performance Indicators (KPIs)	Calculations	Target	What does it mean?	Frequency
1 - CLIENT DEVELOPMENT				
1-CD (a) New Client Conversion Rate (%)	Number of New Clients / Number of Potential Clients	≥ X%	Effectively convert clients	Monthly
1-CD (b) Client Referral Rate (%)	New Clients referred from Existing Client / Total New Clients	≥ X%	Organic client growth	Annually | Quarterly
1-CD (c) Prospect Client Pipeline (#)	Total Number of Prospective Clients / Attorney	≥ #	Sufficient number of potential clients	Monthly
1-CD (d) Adjusted Prospect Pipeline ($)	Total Adjusted Value of Prospective Clients' Matters/ Attorney	≥ $X	Sufficient potential revenue from potential clients	Monthly

Inputs:
1. Client Calls
2. In-Person meetings
3. Total New Clients (or Matters)
4. New Clients Referred by Existing or Former Clients
5. Number of Prospective Clients (Leads)
6. Number of Attorneys
7. Adjusted Value (Prospect Pipeline)

1-CD(a):New Client Conversion Rate
3/(1+2) where 1+2= potential clients

1-CD(b):Client Referral Rate
4/3

1-CD(c): Prospect Client Pipeline
5/6

1-CD(d): Adjusted Prospect Pipeline
7/6

APPENDIX C

Comprehensive KPI Listing—KPI 2: Client Acquisition Costs

App. C — LAW FIRM KEY PERFORMANCE INDICATORS

Key Performance Indicators (KPIs)	Calculations	Target	What does it mean?	Frequency
2 - CLIENT ACQUISITION COSTS				
2-CAC (a) Client Acquisition Cost (CAC) ($)	Sales and marketing spend + opportunity cost of staff or lawyer time/# New Clients	≤ $X	Spend to acquire clients	Monthly
2-CAC (b) Upsell Rate (%)	Number of New Matters with Existing Clients/All New Matters	≥ X%	Organic growth	Quarterly
2-CAC (c) Client Lifetime or Annual Value (CLV) ($)	Cumulative Revenue / Client	≥ $X	Total value of client	Annually
2-CAC (d) CLV to CAC Ratio (#)	CLV / CAC	≥ 1X	Revenue exceeds client acquisition costs	Annually

APPENDICES

Inputs:
1. Advertising, Sales, & Marketing Costs
2. Number of Billable Hours in Client Development
3. Average Billing Rate in Client Development
4. Total New Clients
5. New Matters from Existing Clients
6. Total New Matters
7. Cumulative Revenue (Client, Matter, or Firm)
8. Total Clients Served

2-CAC(a): Client Acquisition Cost
(1+(2 X 3))/4

2-CAC(b): Upsell Rate
5/6

2-CAC(c): Client Lifetime or Annual Value (CLV)
7/8

2-CAC(d): CLV to CAC Ratio
2-CAC(c) / 2-CAC(a)

APPENDIX D

Comprehensive KPI Listing—KPI 3: Productivity

Key Performance Indicators (KPIs)		Calculations	Target	What does it mean?	Frequency
3 - PRODUCTIVITY					
3-PROD (a)	Client Pipeline (#)	Number of Active Clients /Attorney	≥ #	Sufficient pipeline of client work	Monthly
3-PROD (b)	Revenue per Matter ($)	Total Revenue / Number of Open Matters	≥ $X	Right client size	Monthly
3-PROD (c)	Rent Expense (%)	Total Rent Expense/ Total Revenue	≤ X%	Efficient use of facilities	Quarterly
3-PROD (d)	Attorney Leverage (%)	Total $ Billings of All Attorneys / Total Billable $	≥ X%	Attorney efficiency	Quarterly
3-PROD (e)	Paralegal Leverage (%)	Total $ Billings of All Paralegals / Total Billable $	≥ X%	Paralegal efficiency	Quarterly
3-PROD (f)	Attorneys' Productivity (%)	Total # Hours Billed by Attorney / Available Hours (2000) X #Attorneys	≥ X%	Sufficient amount of client work	Quarterly	Annually
3-PROD (g)	Paralegals' Productivity (%)	Total # Hours Billed by Paralegal / Available Hours (2000) X #Paralegals	≥ X%	Sufficient amount of client work	Quarterly	Annually

APPENDICES App. D

Inputs:
1. Total Number of Active Firm Clients
2. Total Attorneys
3. Total Revenue for All Matters
4. Number of Open Matters
5. Rent Expense
6. Total Revenue per Financial Statements
7. Total Billings by All Attorneys
8. Total Billings by Firm
9. Total Billings by All Paralegals
10. Total Number of Billed Attorney Hours
11. Total Number of Attorneys
12. Total Hours Available for Attorneys
13. Total Number of Billed Paralegal Hours
14. Total Number of Paralegals
15. Total Hours Available for Paralegals

3-PROD(a): Client Pipeline (#)
1/2

2-PROD(b): Revenue per Matter (#)
3/4

2-PROD(c): Rent Expense (%)
5/6

2-PROD(d): Attorney Leverage (%)
7/8

2-PROD(e): Paralegal Leverage (%)
9/8

2-PROD(f): Attorney Productivity (%)
10/(11 X 12)

2-PROD(g): Paralegal Productivity (%)
13/(14 X 15)

APPENDIX E

Comprehensive KPI Listing—KPI 4: Profitability

App. E — Law Firm Key Performance Indicators

Key Performance Indicators (KPIs)	Calculations	Target	What does it mean?	Frequency
4 - PROFITABILITY				
4-PROF (a) Return on Owner Equity (Investment) (ROI) (%)	Owner Compensation / Gross Revenue	≥ X%	Profit in terms of ROI	Annually
4-PROF (b) Contribution Margin ($)	Gross Revenue less Direct Cost (at firm, department, or matter level)	≥ $X	Profitable Matters	Monthly
4-PROF (c) Profitability Margin (%)	Total Net Income / Total Revenue	≥ X%	Profitable Firm	Monthly
4-PROF (d) Payroll Ratio (%)	Total Payroll Costs / Total Revenue	≤ X%	Personnel costs levels are at standard	Monthly
4-PROF (e) Overhead Ratio (%)	(Total Expense less Total Payroll Costs) / Total Revenue	≤ X%	Overhead costs are at standard	Monthly
4-PROF (f) Aging Tolerance (%)	Total Collected within 60 days / Total billings	≥ X%	Efficient collection	Monthly
4-PROF (g) Work in Progress (WIP) Lockup Days (#)	365 Days / WIP Turnover (WIP / Average WIP balance)	≤ X	Average days to until WIP time billed	Monthly
4-PROF (h) Accounts Receivable (A/R) Lockup Days (#)	365 Days / A/R Turnover (Billings / Average A/R balance)	≤ X	Average days to collect the A/R	Monthly
4-PROF (i) Year over Year Revenue Growth (%)	Current Year Total Gross Revenue / Prior Year Total Gross Revenue	≥ X%	Growth rate	Quarterly
4-PROF (j) Revenue per Employee ($)	Collected Revenue / # Employees	≥ $X	Right number of Employees	Annually
4-PROF (k) Revenue per Attorney ($)	Collected Revenue / # Attorneys	≥ $X	Right number of Attorneys	Annually

APPENDICES App. E

Inputs:
1. Owner or Partner Compensation
2. Total Annual Gross Revenue
3. Total Monthly Gross Revenue
4. Monthly Direct Costs
5. Number of Matters
6. Monthly Net Income
7. Revenue Per Financial Statements
8. Monthly Payroll Costs
9. Monthly Expenses (Nonpayroll)
10. Accounts Receivable Greater than 60 Days
11. Total Monthly Firm Billings
12. Unbilled (WIP) for the Month
13. WIP Balance—Beginning of the Period
14. WIP Balance—End of the Period
15. Billings for the Month
16. A/R—Beginning of the Period
17. A/R—End of the Period
18. Current Year Gross Revenue by Month
19. Prior Year Gross Revenue by Month
20. Average Number of Annual Employees
21. Average Number of Attorneys

4-PROF(a):Return on Owner Equity (Investment) (%)
1/2

4-PROF(b):Contribution Margin ($)
(3-4)/5

4-PROF(c):Profitability Margin (%)
6/7

4-PROF(d):Payroll Ratio (%)
8/7

4-PROF(e):Overhead Ratio (%)
9/7

4-PROF(f):Aging Tolerance (%)
10/11

4-PROF(g): Work in Progress (WIP) Lockup Days (#)

$$\text{Days in period} / (12/(\tfrac{(13+14)}{2}))$$

4-PROF(h): Accounts Receivable (A/R) Lockup Days (#)

$$\text{Days in period} / (15/(\tfrac{(16+17)}{2}))$$

4-PROF(i): Year over Year Revenue Growth (%)
18/19

4-PROF(j): Revenue per Employee ($)
18/20

4-PROF(k): Revenue per Attorney ($)
18/21

APPENDIX F

Comprehensive KPI Listing—KPI 5: Performance

App. F — Law Firm Key Performance Indicators

Key Performance Indicators (KPIs)		Calculations	Target	What does it mean?	Frequency
S- PERFORMANCE					
S-PERF (a)	Billings Collected by Attorney (%)	Total $ Collected by Attorney / Total $ Billings by Attorney	≥X%	Attorney realization	Monthly
S-PERF (b)	Billings Collected by Paralegal (%)	Total $ Collected by Paralegal / Total $ Billings by Paralegal	≥X%	Paralegal realization	Monthly
S-PERF (c)	Net Collection by Attorney ($/Hour)	Total Collected $ by Attorney / Available Hours	≥ $X	Attorney effectiveness	Monthly
S-PERF (d)	Net Collection by Paralegal ($/Hour)	Total Collected $ by Paralegal / Available Hours	≥ $X	Paralegal effectiveness	Monthly
S-PERF (e)	Hourly Billings by Attorney ($/Hour)	Total $ Billings by Attorney/Actual Billed Hours	≥ $X	Attorney efficiency	Monthly
S-PERF (f)	Hourly Billings by Paralegal ($/Hour)	Total $ Billings by Paralegal/Actual Billed Hours	≥ $X	Paralegal efficiency	Monthly
S-PERF (g)	Hourly Revenue Collected by Attorney ($/Hour)	Total $ Collected by Attorney / Actual Billed Hours	≥ $X	Attorney realization	Annually
S-PERF (h)	Hourly Revenue Collected by Paralegal ($/Hour)	Total $ Collected by Paralegal / Actual Billed Hours	≥ $X	Paralegal realization	Annually

Inputs:
1. Dollars Collected by Timekeeper
2. Dollars Billed by Timekeeper
3. Available Hours by Timekeeper
4. Actual Billed Hours by Timekeeper

5-PERF (a) Billings Collected by Attorney & (b) Billings Collected by Paralegal
1/2

5-PERF (c)Net Collection by Attorney & (d) Net Collection by Paralegal
1/3

5-PERF (e)Hourly Billings by Attorney & (f)Hourly Billings by Paralegal
2/4

5-PERF (g)Hourly Revenue Collected by Attorney & (h)Hourly Revenue Collected by Paralegal
1/4

APPENDIX G

Comprehensive KPI Listing—KPI 6: Client Experience

App. G LAW FIRM KEY PERFORMANCE INDICATORS

Key Performance Indicators (KPIs)	Calculations	Target	What does it mean?	Frequency
6. CLIENT EXPERIENCE				
6-CE (a) Net Promoter Score (NPS) (%)	% of clients who are promoters less % of clients who are detractors	≥X%	Clients value services	Monthly
6-CE (b) Client Service Recovery Rate (%)	% of NPS detractor or neutral responses that move to promoter/detractor & neutral	≥X%	Resolve Client experience issues	Quarterly
6-CE (c) Bar Complaints (#)	# of Complaints filed with Bar Association	X	Complaints resolution	Monthly

APPENDICES   App. G

Inputs:
1. NPS Survey Total Number of Responses
2. NPS Survey Total Number of Promoters
3. NPS Survey Total Number of Neutrals
4. NPS Survey Total Number of Detractors
5. Repeat NPS Survey Total Number of Responses
6. Repeat NPS Survey Total Number from Neutral to Promoter
7. Repeat NPS Survey Total Number from Detractor to Promoter
8. Total Number of Bar Complaints Received

6-CE(a): Net Promoter Score
2/1—4/1

6-CE(b): Client Services Recovery Rate
(6+7)/5

6-CE(c): Number of Bar Complaints
8

APPENDIX H

Comprehensive KPI Listing—KPI 7: Firm Culture

App. H — Law Firm Key Performance Indicators

Key Performance Indicators (KPIs)		Calculations	Target	What does it mean?	Frequency
7. FIRM CULTURE					
7-FM (a)	Average Work Climate Satisfaction (#)	Total Work Climate Survey Score (Scale 1-5) / # Surveys	≥ X	Positive work environment	Quarterly
7-FM (b)	Employee Involvement (%)	Number of Employees participating in company events/Total number of employees	≥ X%	Engaged employees	Quarterly
7-FM (c)	Leverage (%)	Total Managing Partner (MP) Billings / Total Billings	≤ X%	Growth Potential	Quarterly
7-FM (d)	Annual Turnover (%)	# of Attorneys & Paralegals Departed/Max. # of Attorneys & Paralegals over the Year	≤ X%	Employee satisfaction	Annually

APPENDICES   App. H

Inputs:
1. Total All Work Climate Survey Scores Divided by Number of Questions
2. Total Number of Surveys Completed
3. Total Number of Employees Participating in Events
4. Total Number of Events
5. Total Number of Employees
6. Managing Partner Billings
7. Total Billings
8. Number of Associates and Paralegals Who Left in the Year
9. Maximum Number of Associates and Paralegals over the Year

7-FC(a)
1/2

7-FC(a)
3/(4 x 5)

7-FC(a)
6/7

7-FC(a)
8/9

APPENDIX I
Implementation Workshop Outline

First, know your audience. Are you an attorney or administrator attempting to have your firm implement KPIs, or an outside consultant or accountant? Regardless, the size of the firm is very important.

Next, understand the attorneys' motivation for the practice of law and why they wish to implement a KPI framework.

Then, you can design the day as a kick-off for a customized KPI workshop with an overall goal of an action plan to implement the framework. That includes explaining the framework in the context of the firm and educating the partners, managing partners, attorneys, or paralegals in addition to any assistants or administrative staff. Each firm will be at a different starting place and will also approach implementation differently. Some may wish to implement the entire framework, while others may choose several KPI areas to address problem areas first, or even decide to adopt two KPI metrics from each of the seven areas.

Regardless, this workshop should be highly interactive to succeed. Ensure the decision makers are involved at the correct level and that those who will implement the KPIs are present.

Homework:

Request two years of past financial statements and any existing KPIs.

Ask each partner what they feel are the top three weak areas.

Request a list of all technology currently used and a list of websites and social media accounts.

Workshop

Walk through the typical client's or clients' lifecycle to create the client workflow and validate the pain points previously submitted.

Discuss how to apply the KPI framework to each step and the resources needed.

List the gaps in process, technology, and know-how.

Agree on approach that best matches the firm.

Follow-Up List

Excel KPI workbook—unless the legal practice management

system allows customization to create a KPI dashboard, Excel can be used and linked to systems to avoid data reentry as best as can be done without an integrated dashboard.

Data & Sources—Identify all sources for the data; who will gather and when; and find and solve for any gaps.

Commit to a monthly review for the first year and continuous improvement.

APPENDIX J
Technology Resources*

I did hear a lawyer at an ABA conference presentation state that not having a practice management system was the same as committing malpractice. I believe he was referring to the ability to calendar deadlines, protect client information, and avoid mistakes in practicing law. However, I think you can extend that thinking to the use of technology to improve legal service delivery efficiency and thus improve affordable access to the law.

When shopping for technology the same principles apply as when setting up your KPI framework—keep it super simple (KISS). The key principle is ensuring that systems integrate, and not just in a superficial fashion. In other words, you want to log on to one system to run your business, not hopping on and off multiple systems and worrying about remembering to export. It almost goes without saying that double data entry is taboo.

Interoperability is the step beyond integration, and in this context, it means that without an outside intervention, data and systems operate together. For example, the legal practice management (LPM) system should have time and billing building. Then, the LPM automatically generates billing and accounts receivable information for financial reporting, management, and KPI purposes. It would then be a requirement to have the accounting system properly integrated. Specifically, the integration with either QuickBooks or Xero must be an automatic push of the billing information from the practice management system to populate the financials.

For small firm KPIs, there are limited options as far as affordable platforms or dashboards. Large firms can afford business intelligence (BI) systems that pull all the data from various systems. Practice management systems should be home to the KPI dashboard for firms.

When attorneys use these systems, they can automate the tasks that do not require any professional judgment and allow for efficiencies. Below is a listing of some of the technologies that

---

*This is only a list of resources and is not exhaustive, nor complete, nor an endorsement by the author.

small firms can examine. Evolve Law's Legal Technology Toolkit (LTTK) is found at http://evolvelawnow.com/legal-tech-toolkit/ and includes many of these resources. I am cofounder of Evolve Law and founder of Traklight.com but have no financial stake in these other resources. As stated in the footnote, this is simply an alphabetical listing, and I am not promoting or being compensated for including these companies in this appendix. My goal is for attorneys to explore how technology can augment their practice, whether in the backend, with administrative work, or with client-facing technologies.

Website Development
One400
LawLytics

Marketing:
Clear View Social
Findlaw
Foxwordy
Hubspot (CRM)
Infusionsoft (CRM)
Lexicata (CRM legal)
Local Lawyer Guide
Salesforce for Small Business | Legal (CRM Legal)

Client Interview Automation
Traklight Pro (Business, Intellectual Property, Employment, Startup & Venture)
Wevorce (Family Law)

Filing Automation
Alt Legal—Intellectual Property
Cognate—Intellectual Property
Valcu—Incorporation

Client Relationship Management
Hubspot (CRM)
Infusionsoft (CRM)
Lexicata (CRM legal)
Salesforce for Small Business | Legal (CRM Legal)

Legal Practice Management, Time & Billing, Research
Firm Central—Westlaw embedded

Calendaring External to Practice Management System
Youcanbookme.com

Court | Litigation
Allegory Law
Concept Red
Docket Alarm
FactBox
LiveDeposition
ServeManager

Document Automation
iDisclose (Venture Funding)
PatDek (USPTO)
Sharewave (Cap Table Management)

E-discovery
Cicayda
eBrevia

E-billing
Simple Legal
E-signature
Docusign

Project Management
Asana
SmartSheet
LexProjex

Time, Billing, & Accounting
Firm Central
Fundbox—Collections

Accounting & Payroll
QuickBooks
Xero
Freshbooks

APPENDIX K

Intersection with Firm Central & KPI Implementation Plan

Firm Central is Thomson Reuters' legal practice management (LPM) system that includes a time and billing module plus client portal and storage. As of June 2016, the LPM system does not include a KPI dashboard but does provide data for the KPI framework in this book.

The Home tab accesses the following technologies to help with the client workflow:

- Calendar (with Outlook integration);
- Practical Law includes Practice Notes, Standard Documents, Checklists, and 50-State Q&A;
- Thomson Reuters WestLaw—Legal Research; and
- Tools—Document Builder and Hosted Case Notebook.

Integrations:

Outlook: Using the "Events in Firm Central" calendar option, users can execute a two-way sync between Firm Central and Outlook Calendar. Two-way means the data goes to and from Firm Central. Users can also copy e-mails from Outlook into Firm Central using the folder system or a "Copy to Firm Central" button. This will allow users to use Outlook to send out the KPI 6-CE Net Promoter Score survey e-mails and keep track of it within Firm Central.

QuickBooks:

You can sync your time and billing data one-way from Firm Central to QuickBooks (QB) using the QB icon. The information is not automatically sent and only goes one-way, from Firm Central to QB. For those technology readers, the integration uses QuickBooks SDK, the recommended exchange technology.

Reports:

Exportable reports that can be converted to Excel files to ultimately link to the firm's KPI dashboard. The number of clients and matters can be mined for client development, client acquisition costs, productivity, and so on. The time and billing report will capture the nonbillable time for client acquisition costs and, of course, the information needed on the time and billing side for profitability and performance.

The Firm Central time and billing system generates the following reports:

Reports

- **Time by Matter or Client**
  Unbilled and billed time for a matter or client
- **Time by User**
  Unbilled and billed time for one or all users
- **Expense by Matter**
  Expenses for one or all matters
- **Account Receivable**
  Outstanding Accounts Receivable
- **Trust Account Balances**
  Trust Account balances by date
- **Collection Realization by Matter**
  Collection realization for one matter or all matters
- **Collection Realization by Client**
  Collection realization for one client or all clients
- **Write Off's**
  Write offs, Credits & Discounts for one client or all clients

The Accounts Receivable (A/R) report shows the aged outstanding receivables balances by client (or matter) and is, therefore, useful for KPI 4-PROF(f) Aging Tolerance. You can also set up the system to show overdue A/R: for example, a listing of all invoices over 20 days old. Unbilled time (WIP) can also be shown by matter or client, at the timekeeper level, for a month or other periods of time.

Billings data comes from the time reports, and the collection dollars by client or matter is on the collection realization reports. At this time, the collection realization reports are not available by timekeeper. However, a report on write-offs by lead attorney is in development as Firm Central moves towards improved KPI reporting for small law.

APPENDIX L

Small Law Firm KPI/Benchmarking Practices Survey Questions (June 2016)

Research Purpose:
- Better understand how/if small law firms currently measure and track their business metrics

Research Scope:
- Thomson Reuter Customer Panel poll

Research Questions

1. How many attorneys work at your firm?
    a. 1
    b. 2-3
    c. 4-6
    d. 7-10
    e. 11-20
    f. 21-29
    g. 30+
2. What is your role?
    a. Associate
    b. Paralegal
    c. Partner / Managing Partner
    d. Solo Attorney
    e. Office Manager/Administrator
    f. Other
3. How many support staff (nonattorneys) work at your firm?
    a. 0
    b. 1
    c. 2-3
    d. 4-6
    e. 7-10
    f. 11-20
    g. 21-29
    h. 30+
4. Do you use Key Performance Indicators (KPIs), beyond traditional number of hours billed, in your practice? This

may include metrics such as number of matters, number of new clients, or dollar value of new business.
Yes or No
  a. If yes, which of the KPIs (check all that apply)
Client satisfaction, for example Net Promoter Score
Cost of client development or acquisition
Pipeline dollar value per attorney
Aged/overdue accounts receivable (firm or attorney)
Collected billings by attorney
Matter profitability
Budget vs. actual
Other (fill in)

5. What is your one best indicator of firm profitability at this time?
Take-home amount at month's end
Actual account balance
Matter profitability
Overall firm cost vs. pipeline/expected revenue
<fill in >

6. Do all your timekeepers have financial goals/targets?
Yes or No
  a. If yes, what targets are set? (check all that apply)
    Hours
    Billings
    Collections
    New clients
    All of the above

7. Do you use billing or accounting software product(s) to track your firm's performance and/or KPIs?
Yes or No
  a. If yes, which one(s)? <fill in >

8. Has your firm profitability grown over the past two years?
Yes or No or Don't Know
  a. If yes, by what amount? <fill in>

APPENDIX M
Resources

Evolve Law website (www.evolvelawnow.com)

QuickBooks for Law Firms, Caren Schwartz, The Sleeter Group, 2014.

Thomson Reuters June 2016 Survey (APPENDIX F)

Thomson Reuters Firm Central

Thomson Reuters Peer Monitor 2015 and 2106 Report on the State of the Legal Market

Thomson Reuters "Stake Out Your Competitive Advantage in a Buyer's Market" 2016 Joint Spring Meeting—May 13, 2016. Matt St. John, J.D. presenter.

Tiny Pulse website (www.tinypulse.com)

Disclaimer—The firm examples in chapters 4 to 10 are not actual client case studies, nor do they represent real firms.